of related interest

Autism Heroes
Portraits of Families Meeting the Challenge
Barbara Firestone, Ph.D.
Photographs by Joe Buissink
Forewords by Teddi Cole and Gary Cole and Catherine Lord, Ph.D.
ISBN 978 1 84310 837 5

Coach Yourself Through the Autism Spectrum
Ruth Knott Schroeder
Foreword by Linda Miller
ISBN 978 1 84905 801 8

Hope for the Autism Spectrum
A Mother and Son Journey of Insight and Biomedical Intervention
Sally Kirk
ISBN 978 1 84310 894 8

Hints and Tips for Helping Children with Autism Spectrum Disorders
Useful Strategies for Home, School, and the Community
Dion E. Betts and Nancy J. Patrick
ISBN 978 1 84310 896 2

A Spectrum of Light

Inspirational Interviews with Families Affected by Autism

Francesca Bierens

Jessica Kingsley Publishers
London and Philadelphia

First published in 2010
by Jessica Kingsley Publishers
116 Pentonville Road
London N1 9JB, UK
and
400 Market Street, Suite 400
Philadelphia, PA 19106, USA

www.jkp.com

Copyright © Francesca Bierens 2010

Library of Congress Cataloging in Publication Data
A CIP catalog record for this book is available from the Library of Congress

British Library Cataloguing in Publication Data
A CIP catalogue record for this book is available from the British Library

ISBN 978 1 84905 013 5

Printed and bound in the United States by
Thomson-Shore, 7300 West Joy Road, Dexter, MI 48130

*To Dad, who taught me
the importance of listening.*

This book is dedicated to all the families who have children with special needs and the children and adults themselves, especially those with autism spectrum disorder.

It is also dedicated to the quest to make every community throughout the world more understanding and accepting of people who are different; to assist communities to acquire the wisdom to see that all people have an important contribution to make in their unique way to the colour of our world.

Contents

Acknowledgements

First, I would like to acknowledge the people who contributed to this book. It has been a privilege to be able to share your experiences. My most sincere thanks to you all.

I would like to thank Kathryn Warren for her patient and practical assistance and the late Rudi and Bailey Bisenberger for their support. Also many thanks to Sue Robertson for her incredible knowledge, and Lynette Buchan for her much valued assistance. I must thank Eila Wild for her wisdom, Ai-Na Khor for her assistance and support, Marilyn Burrows, Janeane Campbell and Avril Warren, for their enthusiasm and encouragement, and Pat Nalleweg for her practical guidance.

Special thanks to Heather Buckingham and Sonia Gould who have maintained an active interest and encouraged me with this project throughout the years.

My heartfelt thanks to Jessica Kingsley Publishers who also saw the importance of what these families have to share, especially Lily Morgan who has patiently guided me to the completion of this book.

Preface

The purpose of this book is to provide families who have a child diagnosed with autism spectrum disorder with feelings of hope for a positive future. It is also my intention to provide people who do not have first hand experience, with increased understanding of how autism affects the child and the family.

At the time of the original interviews, I had no idea of the level of diversity that I would see in the children when they became adults. Fourteen years ago, when the families volunteered to contribute to the book, no thought or criteria were even considered in regards to the individual abilities of their children.

When the original interviews were carried out, it was only five years after the 1989 'Education Act' which entitled children with a disability to enrol at mainstream schools. So although some schools had been enrolling children with special needs in their schools prior to this, many schools were still getting used to the concept of 'inclusion'. Over the years between the interviews, many terms used by the parents have changed. 'Meltdowns' are now used more frequently to describe temper tantrums, and the term Asperger Syndrome is now a recognized diagnosis.

I am indebted to the families who contributed to this book, for sharing their knowledge so willingly and helping to answer many of the questions often asked by new parents.

Worthy of note is the fact that, of the seven families, all but one marriage is still intact and that one is still a supportive relationship with the son living with his dad. So when parents of newly diagnosed children are warned that most marriages in that situation break up, review that thought. From the experiences of these families, that is not always true.

Throughout the many years that I have worked with children with autism spectrum disorder, it is the families who have been my most valuable resource. I have the greatest admiration and respect for the parents with whom I have worked. Apart from the children themselves, it is the parents who have been my greatest teachers and I have learnt an enormous amount from them.

I am honoured to have become the guardian of this book. It is not my book. The book belongs to the people who have contributed to it. I have merely listened to their experiences and made sure that they were shared. This book has taken me in the most interesting directions that I would never have believed. My wish is that the reader is as enlightened by the experiences shared, and learns as much as I have.

Introduction

This book consists of a series of interviews, first carried out in 1994 with ten families, all of whom had a child diagnosed with autism spectrum disorder. The 'children' then ranged in ages from two years of age to an adult of 30 years. All those who contributed to the book did so voluntarily and only two of the families were previously known to me.

Fourteen years later, I had the very good fortune of being able to speak with seven of those original ten families. Of the remaining three families, one had left the country, one had moved to another city and one had left the area and was unable to be located.

I am very grateful to these seven families for their willingness to provide a follow-up interview all these years later. To my absolute delight and great excitement, two of the 'children', who have now grown into young adults, also wanted to contribute.

For the purposes of confidentiality, the children's names have been changed. For the same reason, references to specific places such as schools have also been omitted.

CHAPTER 1

'Life does get easier'

In the early stages following the child's diagnosis, it is difficult for many families to imagine that life will get better. As victories are won, however, progress is made from a time when behaviours and obsessions made life difficult. Although there continue to be the challenges, parents usually discovered for themselves that life with their child certainly does improve.

MOTHER OF PETER: 17 YEARS

Life's just so much easier now. I want other mothers to know that it does get easier. When Peter was younger, we could hardly take him anywhere. He didn't like high buildings. He was terrified of getting into a lift. You couldn't take him to the movies, which was hard on my other son.

Peter is essentially happy now. You really just have to have patience. It would've been so much easier then if I knew he was going to outgrow his fears and phobias. At the time I never looked ahead. I didn't see the future. I didn't see things changing, whereas now you can tell people with two-year-olds that things are going to get better.

PARENTS OF JENNY: 2 YEARS

Father: Sleeping-wise, she always had a really disturbed sleeping pattern and sort of woke up for no apparent reason. Well, most kids wake up in the middle of the night, but she just wanted attention the whole time. We would, on average, have got up to her two to three times a night. When she was sick or was upset it sometimes got worse. Some nights for the first year and a half, I could have counted on one hand the number of nights where she slept the whole night without requiring attention. The worst night that I ever had, I was on duty that night, I had to get out of bed 14 times. That just about killed me but that's the way it goes. Then she started for some reason or another to start sleeping through the night, which was wonderful. We would put her to bed at 6.00pm or 6.30pm and she would be asleep right the way through.

MOTHER OF PETER: 17 YEARS

The most important thing is to get plenty of sleep. If you don't, then it's hard to maintain a sense of humour. But it changes you. It makes you more outgoing because you're always having to stand up for your child all the time. It really brings you out of yourself.

PARENTS OF ELEANOR: 7 YEARS

Mother: The best piece of advice I ever received was from a friend, another parent. It could only have come from another parent who had experienced grief and it was tremendously useful. She said to me one day when I was very upset, 'It's as if you're in a tremendously rough sea right now. You are way down the bottom of a trough and you'll go up to a massive high. Then you'll go right down and then you'll go up to another massive high and then you'll go deep down again. But every time you go up, the high will be slightly less high and when you go down, the trough will not be so deep. What you're aiming for now is not so low and not so high, but just little waves.'

I found that really useful and I realized as time went by that it gets slightly better with each low and you never go as low as that first deep depression again.

MOTHER OF JOSEPH: 7 YEARS

Autism brings out really good qualities in parents. It puts your life in perspective a bit. It does make you see things from a different angle and have different priorities. I feel proud of what we've achieved because it is something you achieve. It's not something that just happens. You have to work really hard at making a life for him. It's not as it is with the other children. Wherever Joseph goes you have to fight for every little thing and create a life for him because people would prefer it if they didn't have to know about it.

I really feel that he's got a fulfilling life at the moment and a very normal sort of life, which is important to us. We want him to enjoy and have a fulfilling and rich life and I think he's got that.

PARENTS OF RICHARD: 11 YEARS

Father: Richard doesn't panic as much as he used to. He can seek help if he needs to. He likes routine things. He likes bringing the washing in. For a while he was making stewed apples and he was peeling the apples every night. He was really very clever with it. We have a two-litre glass bowl and he could peel the exact amount of apples that, when chopped up, would fit into the bowl.

He gets upset if he loses familiar things such as if his towel goes missing or if part of his clothing can't be found. But you can usually get him to accept it. If you talk to him, he will calm down. As far as the activities during the day are concerned, you can vary them more easily than you used to. It's been gradual.

PARENTS OF ALEX: 7 YEARS

Mother: We went to the supermarket on Saturday which was out of routine. So we didn't go around the supermarket the same way. There wasn't a problem. And when I got everything in the boot of the car, I said to Alex, 'Now you put your things in your bag, and I'll take everything else.' (We always talk to her normally. We always talk to her as if she understands and maybe a percentage of what she understands is increasing. It still depends. She has good days and bad days.) And she did. She picked out her wine gums and her Coke and her special things that she had got for her and put them into her bag.

Father: Normally I let them get their own things. They get a bottle of Coke and they're allowed a packet of chips. But on Monday (they had had enough last week when we were on holiday), we just walked straight past them. She indicated she wanted to pick them up but I just said, 'No' and that was the end of it. Normally we would have had a tantrum in the past, but not now.

PARENTS OF JENNY: 2 YEARS

Father: On the weekends, I'll be doing a couch potato routine, just relaxing. You can see by Jenny, she's sort of pacing around and getting more and more bored. Usually when she's really bored she will start opening cupboards and pulling things out and that's when she's destructive and wanting attention. She gets bored really quickly. She loves water, absolutely loves water. She'll stay in there for hours, the jacuzzi as well, although it's only in the last three or four weeks that she has actually started staying in there and relaxing. Just sitting in the jacuzzi rather than splashing, getting in and out, jumping around. In fact at one stage it was dangerous because she would just walk out into the middle and just sink, but she loves the jacuzzi. She loves buckets. If you put a bucket of water out in the sun she will just play with that for ages too.

She loves playing outside. It's great in the summer, you can just leave her and she will just wander around. We're going to get a sandpit out the back for her.

FAMILY OF DAVID: 8 YEARS

Mother: David went through a stage at three years of age that he just screamed. He would carry on playing but he would just scream.

Grandmother: He used to get so frustrated. He used to watch our mouths and try to make the sound. We thought he was hearing things differently. His mum took him to get his hearing tested and I could hear him screaming several rooms away. There was nothing wrong with his hearing.

Mother: When he was a preschooler, he just played on his own. He used to lie down when he first got a little car and spin the wheels around. He could do that all day. I used to have to put David in a playpen. He was constantly hitting his baby brother. He stopped head-banging when he was about three and a half.

Grandmother: He used to spend a lot of time spinning around and around. He hated being touched. Even as a baby, he used to sit away from you. He never ever cuddled in. He was a stiff baby.

His mother taught him to give us a cuddle. He wouldn't kiss you. We never ever pushed him. I know it was difficult for him. His mother would say, 'Go and give Nana and Grandad a hug.' He would back into you and that was how he acknowledged you. He would have been about six.

PARENTS OF JENNY: 2 YEARS

Father: She wouldn't sleep unless she was in bed with us. She wouldn't go to sleep. That was a bad habit that we got into. So we plonked her in her own bed for about a week. We had three nights of hell, crying. The doctor told us we had to do it and I'm glad we did. That was learning from mistakes.

Three nights of screaming and it stopped. She decided it wasn't worth it. In the old days you couldn't get her near the bedroom. Now once it's bed time, you get her juice ready and she'll actually run into the room and climb into bed and lie down ready for her juice. That's happened in the last month.

FAMILY OF DAVID: 8 YEARS

Mother: It wasn't until he was about five and a half, when he started school, that he started noticing people. He used to show his affection towards us by steering his face into a certain expression and coming towards us.

I remember the first spontaneous affection was when he was five, he said 'Goodnight' to me. That was the first thing he said without a prompt. I remember I wrote that down because I was so impressed that he said 'Goodnight'.

At six and a half years he was 'de-labelled'. Two psychologists 'interviewed' him and talked to him over a period of three hours. They now say he is a very unusual child, but is no longer autistic. He certainly has come a long way from the head-banging, screaming, obsessive child we used to have.

Even to me, as a highly critical parent, he really does appear to be 'normal', whatever that may mean. He still tends to take things literally and has trouble seeing the point of a joke, but otherwise seems just like any other boy his age.

PARENTS OF RICHARD: 11 YEARS

Mother: He's got a sense of humour now and that's fairly recent. He's only just started watching television for enjoyment. He goes to school and talks about what was on the night before and he can go into quite a bit of detail about what happened. So that's quite exciting.

Father: Richard has had personally and mentally to work on everything himself and he has succeeded. His improvement seems to go hand in hand with consistent all-round stimulation. Consistent is the operative word and he's happy.

He's still developing. He hasn't stopped developing and he doesn't look like stopping. That's the exciting part of it for us. But for me he's a pleasure to have. I'm happy with him, whatever stage he's at. We like to see his little victories coming all the time and we look forward to the next one. We enjoy Richard.

CHAPTER 2

'We're a family – we go where she can go'

The child with autism spectrum disorder is a treasured member of the family and has a rightful place in it. Criticism and exclusion of the child by other family members or friends is hurtful for both the child and the parents. Having a child with autism does, however, usually require the family to make certain adaptations, which have in fact frequently been of benefit to the other children in the family.

PARENTS OF RICHARD: 11 YEARS

Father: The two younger boys have gained from having Richard as their brother because we have made the effort to go out, and all the time we're looking for more creative ideas as to what to do with the children, always speaking positively. The boys gain from that.

Mother: We haven't really made all that many adaptations. Richard has always been there. He's very easy. The more we've had to help him, the more it's helped the two younger boys. We've almost had to be extrovert in the way we teach Richard, so they've had more input than they would have. Six years ago, you couldn't leave Richard with just anyone. Certainly not a babysitter, so we tended to stay home more and we've done more as the five of us.

FAMILY OF JOHN: 8 YEARS

Father: I think in some ways probably having John in the family means it works like glue for the rest of the family. We have to do things as a family. The girls will go out and do things with other children in the town, but John is a handful for anybody so it's understandable that he doesn't get invited to other people's places. It does happen occasionally. So we do tend to do things as a family because of that and that's the positive side of it.

MOTHER OF PETER: 17 YEARS

Peter adores his father, they are very close. Also his brother is great with him, takes him to the movies, to restaurants with his friends. He has no inhibitions when it comes to Peter.

PARENTS OF ALEX: 7 YEARS

Mother: From the family perspective, the closer friends we've got are the ones with children with special needs. It still tends to be they're the ones you mix with more than anybody else because there is a common bond and you are not really very welcome in other people's homes. It's not that they're unwelcoming, it's just that they choose not to invite us as a family. So over the years the autism has been very isolating for us as a family. And there are simply some houses that we would not choose to go back to. You have to work at not becoming isolated.

FAMILY OF JOHN: 8 YEARS

Mother: As much as possible we do things as a family anyway. Some things we undertake may be a bit too ambitious and they end up disastrous, but then other times you take him on an outing and he ends up really good. Then another time you think, 'Well, he may be disastrous, but we may as well go anyway.' I've taken him to the movies three times now. This year is the first year I was ever brave enough to take him to the movies and I chose things I thought he'd like. The first time he did throw a real wobbly. It was really quite disastrous, but the next two times he's been OK.

Most children who come here often do get used to him. It's the first few times that they see him getting angry that they're stunned. But after they've seen it numerous times, they just ignore it.

MOTHER OF PETER: 17 YEARS

My younger brother was really great. He's nine years younger than me and he and his wife have always treated Peter like my other son, like you'd treat any child. They'd pick him up and throw him up in the air and make him squeal with excitement. They haven't lived in this country for about ten years but they'll be coming home next week. Occasionally they might come round, they'd just take Peter with them. Just throw him in the car and take him with them down to the beach or something.

PARENTS OF ALEX: 7 YEARS

Mother: We used to visit my brother and his wife. They have four girls and Alex was never invited to stay in the same room as the other children. She was never invited because of her differences. I used to feel really hurt by that and it really motivated me to say to my husband, 'Over the next couple of years I would like to get to the point where Alex could share a room so that she can be included.' The last time we went to visit them, you have these strokes of genius from time to time, and her sister was invited to stay the night out on the farm with the other children but Alex wasn't. So what I did was say, 'Well, if you're going to have my eldest that night, can we borrow one of your daughters?' who was nearly the same age as Alex. So their daughter came and stayed the night at the motel and it was a treat because it had a heated pool. So we had one of theirs instead of trying to make a point and ask if Alex could stay. We just reversed it and borrowed a child and that worked extremely well.

MOTHER OF JOSEPH: 7 YEARS

When you first have a son like Joseph, I just rushed around doing all these things. You felt like you owed it to him but you end up just getting so worn out. That's the other hard thing. My husband's not as close to his family as I am and that can be quite hard because they judge you. Joseph isn't doing this, it's because you don't believe in him enough. First of all he wasn't autistic, we just weren't good parents. Then finally after a few years, 'Oh, perhaps he is,' because our youngest turned out normal. Now it's just we don't believe in him enough, that's why he hasn't progressed as far.

PARENTS OF ALEX: 7 YEARS

Mother: One of the most heartbreaking things that is happening for me as her mother currently is that Alex actually desperately wants to be like everybody else. Particularly kids who may be a couple of years older than she is. The other night when her sister had a friend to stay over, Alex screamed and screamed and screamed because she was rejected by everybody. The two-year-old didn't want her, the ten-year-olds didn't want her. It's not dissimilar to being a middle sister, not wanted by anybody, but she wasn't wanted because of her autism, not because of where she was placed. And I find her rejection really sad.

MOTHER OF JOSEPH: 7 YEARS

Every time they come down, there's Joseph and they give him a big hug, 'Poor Joseph being stuck in a family like…', you know. You get that kind of feeling. And then they'll take him and, 'I took him and we climbed the trees, very good for him, and I saw this on TV and I'm going to do this and we read stories and I made him do this', as if I never do any of it. 'Poor old Joseph, I'll save him from that wretched home.'

And it hurts you because they don't see the heartache and the hard work and how you would dearly love for him to be doing those things, and it hurts you. You commit your life to this child and all they can do is turn around and say, 'You should be doing this', and 'Why aren't you doing that?' and 'Why not do this new thing that was on some TV programme?' and 'Have you heard about this?' and I'm supposed to pack my bags that night and rush him off to Europe and do it. And because I don't means I don't care about Joseph, that he's not the most important to us. That's quite hard.

PARENTS OF ALEX: 7 YEARS

Mother: My eldest daughter is jealous of Alex. She always has been jealous of Alex, even when she was a brand new baby. Nothing has changed. I still don't think that she understands what autism is. I think she accepts that Alex will always be like that, but I don't think she understands what it does to Alex. She's at the stage where she's beginning to reach puberty and some of Alex's behaviours are simply embarrassing for her and my eldest is very sensitive about how other people perceive her. And there is absolutely nothing we can do to change that.

MOTHER OF PETER: 17 YEARS

The first time (he went for Riding for the Disabled), he was six years old. They put him on a horse and apparently he screamed 'No', like he was so terrified of being put on that horse that he had to speak. He was terrified, he had to communicate somehow. He had to get through to these people. I wasn't there and as a mother you see their fear and take them away from the situation. You calm them down and sometimes maybe you do too much. You've got this amazing communication between the two of you. That's what my older son says to me, 'You treat him like a baby. You do too much for him.' But I suppose, because I had to do it for so long because he couldn't do it, I had to always quieten all his fears he had, quieten him down. People say to me, 'You've got amazing patience.' Well, I'm such an impatient person, I really am. I don't have any patience with hardly anybody, but why do I have it with Peter and no-one else?

I've always had patience with Peter. I also read the books on autism so I kind of knew what he was going through in some way. That they were just fears. He couldn't help his fears. It was something I was meant to do.

PARENTS OF ALEX: 7 YEARS

Mother: It's a common criticism that is quite often thrown at our family that, 'Gosh, you must spend an enormous amount of time with your affected child and your other children must miss out.' I feel quite angry about that criticism. No, they don't all receive equal amounts of attention at any one particular time of the day. One will require more than the other. But over the space of a week, we achieve as good a balance as we're ever going to achieve, because in their own way, the three children are quite demanding. One point that is quite valid, is that my eldest is aware of the amount of 'thinking' time spent on Alex by me. It's actually not on Alex but on autism and the Autistic Association and the demands that are made on me and requests that are made of me by other people, that all seems to be associated with autism. For a large proportion of time it has nothing to do with Alex, but I just wonder if my eldest's perception is that Alex's autism is the same thing. She is jealous of the amount of thinking time and the amount of physical time spent on it. And it is quite intrusive into our family life. We don't believe that she misses out because of Alex and sometimes I wonder if we have compensated her too much. It's very hard to know.

FAMILY OF DAVID: 8 YEARS

Mother: David's younger brother has had a very good effect on David. There's only 19 months between them and he was talking at nine months. So David learnt a lot off his brother. He was encouraging like, 'That's very good block building, David. That's very good.' I'm sure that helped him, having a younger brother rather than an older brother who's going to say, 'I'm not interested in you', but a younger one that sort of looks up to him, who keeps him talking, keeps him active and keeps him interested.

FAMILY OF JOHN: 8 YEARS

Mother: This year, John's ten-year-old sister had a speech competition at school and she chose to do her speech on John. She was practising at home doing it over and over because she had to do it by heart. (She ended up going to the regional competitions.) And John listened. He listened to her saying, 'That is because John is autistic' and she spoke about his obsessions; in fact he learnt it off by heart. And

I thought, 'How is he going to react to this?' So I said to him, 'Is your sister allowed to talk about John at her school?' Sometimes if I really want him to understand, I talk to him in the third person like he does because he seems to understand that better. And he said, 'Yes.' He was really excited about it. He was really keen on it. She would give her speech at home when she was practising, then he would get up and give it too. So for a while he would walk around saying, 'And that is because John is autistic.'

PARENTS OF ALEX: 7 YEARS

Mother: We think we're normal until someone comes to visit and we realize just how many significant minor adjustments we make in the course of the day to accommodate Alex's differences. Things that we consider are normal that aren't. When we had our cousins come to visit, three girls, they fought and squabbled and argued with each other and it was simple normal sibling rivalry. But my daughter was appalled. We don't have that fighting. That fighting is only just starting to happen between my eldest daughter and her little brother. So we may be over-reacting to this jealous issue which might be just normal behaviour of the two girls. Alex is not able to fight back verbally. She fights back physically which is the only way she can do it.

MOTHER OF PETER: 17 YEARS

People don't seem to understand that I could love Peter. I'm sure they don't. They think that he's different. He was born the same way as any other child is born so why would you treat him any different? Why would you love him any different? People don't seem to understand that and they always talk about 'those' people and that really gets to me. 'Those' people, as if they're not really human beings. They're this other breed of people. There's human beings and there's animals and there's insects and there's 'those' people. They're a separate identity again. They don't think of them as just normal people. They're born the same way, just something has gone slightly wrong with their brain and they do things a bit differently and that's the way I see it.

MOTHER OF JOSEPH: 7 YEARS

Not just relatives, well-meaning people would say, 'Oh, did you see that programme on TV?' or 'Did you read about that? It's supposed to do this.' What am I supposed to do? Abandon my other child? Where do I get the money from, and the time? Some people thrive on that sort of thing but I don't really. I just think this is our lot and we've got to make it as good as you can. Joseph is like this and I tend to get upset with people who say I should do that and feel like they're saying Joseph isn't acceptable as he is. I feel that Joseph can be how he is and that's OK. It is OK, we love him for who he is. He doesn't have to be better and he doesn't have to do this this week and that next week and that in a year's time. If he does that's lovely, you feel really pleased and happy. You have a good feeling if he does stuff but if he doesn't, it's not like you feel he's a failure because he's not. He's got a hell of a lot more to deal with than any of us. That's what most of us don't understand. His everyday living is very hard for him to deal with. He copes with it really well. He's got a lot of frustrations and confusion to deal with.

FAMILY OF ALEX: 7 YEARS

Sister: 10 years: It's very hard. Not many other kids at school have an autistic sister, just one other. When Alex squeals in assembly I feel embarrassed. And everyone knows that she's my sister and they always turn to me.

It gets very annoying when people keep coming up and asking questions, 'What's wrong with Alex?' because I've told them again and again. It's very hard to describe. How did she get autism in the first place? It's not easy having a sister who's autistic. It's a bit lonely.

But I am proud of Alex. I don't like it when people tell her off at school. It's not very fair. How would they like to change places with her? If she hits then she should be told off but if the children hit her, they should be told off. One of the teachers doesn't like disabled children touching her so I told her not to be like that.

FAMILY OF DAVID: 8 YEARS

Grandmother: One of the best things I've seen was when a woman was bringing a very handicapped child in a wheelchair up to the school. He was a very handicapped child, physically and mentally, and all the children made a wide berth. David's younger brother went up and said, 'Hello'. It didn't bother him. There is some good out of this. It helped all of us and gave us a better understanding of disabled people.

Parents of Eleanor: 7 years

Mother: Eleanor is part of the family. She's our little girl. She belongs to us. We go where she can go. We don't go on holidays without her. She's one of us and that's part of the corporate responsibility. If Eleanor can't cope, then the family doesn't do it. We move together as a group. Within reason of course, we try to make her sister's life as normal as possible and the same with her brother but generally we all move in a tight unit. There has to be a feeling of family. That's also very important planning for the future, if you can.

CHAPTER 3

'We are not going to hide our children away'

The African proverb, 'It takes a whole village to raise a child' is one often heard referring to the close-knit support structure of the families who have a child with autism spectrum disorder.

It would be wonderful if this could be expanded to mean exactly what the quote says, 'the whole village', including the bus drivers, the librarians, the workers and customers in the supermarkets, rather than just the people who are involved with the child and family such as other families, a teacher, therapist or doctor.

Unfortunately, even in these 'enlightened times', the area of disability is still a very real area of discrimination. As a society, we are generally much more accepting of people with visible differences, such as the person in a wheelchair, or a blind person, especially if they have a dog, it seems. But the child with autism is still a strange and unknown quantity. These usually beautiful children who 'look so normal' (no cane, no wheelchair, no dog!) yet will not respond with a smile when spoken to like all 'good' children should, or tell people their name when asked; who can erupt at any given moment for what appears to be no good reason, except perhaps the supermarket lights were too bright, the noises too piercing… These children can leave people confused and wondering at the 'parenting skills' of the poor mother and father, leaving parents with not just the child's pain and confusion to deal with but also the onslaught of criticism from relatives and strangers alike. Fortunately more and more people these days know better now than to stare at and criticize people for their differences. Maybe one day, with the new, free-thinking generation coming through, we may yet get that village.

PARENTS OF ALEX: 7 YEARS

Mother: There is such a fine line between being normal and not being normal that a disorder is very frightening for people. They have to face that, 'There, but for the grace of God go I' and that is frightening for many people. We've come through a history where people have been tucked away. We're the generation that said, 'Our child has the right to take part in the community that they were born into and that they live in. So we are not going to hide our children away.'

When you introduce a child who has differences, what you also do is ask people to step outside their comfort zone. And there's also the need to allow people time to get over the 'fear factor'. And I think you can only get over the 'fear factor' by a little public education and by simply being there.

MOTHER OF JOSEPH: 7 YEARS

A lot of the stress in having a child like Joseph is not the child, it's society. It's their lack of understanding and their limitations. That's the greatest stress. Sometimes I think if it were just me and Joseph in this world, we'd be fine. It's all these other people who stare at you, or tell you that you should be doing this, or tell him he can't do that. You get where you don't want to go out because you get sick of being bombarded with that sort of stuff.

Sometimes you just get a bit burnt out and haven't got the energy to face another staring person. I just want to cry so I can't even try to explain about Joseph's disability. I just walk away. But then you have a bit of a break and get your energy up and you go back fighting.

PARENTS OF JENNY: 2 YEARS

Father: It would be very nice sometimes for people I know, work mates or even just members of the general public, to actually spend a day in our shoes.

It's very difficult because when somebody says to you, 'Oh, you've got a two and a half year old. How is she?', I say, 'Well, she's a challenge. She's autistic.' Most people don't know what autism is, so they just smile and go, 'Oh yeah.' I think they think you mean 'artistic'. And of course 'Rain Man' has done a few good things but it has also done a number of bad things. I said to somebody the other day that my daughter's autistic and immediately he said, 'Oh, so she can count, can she?' and 'What can she do? What special abilities has she got?'

There's not enough education out there. That just comes down to the basic old fact of money and the ability for people in power to see the need for some sort of National Centre to provide education. We need a group of people within the Health Department System, a parent representative to decide what's best because the public needs to be educated.

MOTHER OF JOSEPH: 7 YEARS

The principal rang the Special Education Service and wanted them to recommend that Joseph wasn't suitable for mainstreaming and have him out of there. That just makes you so angry as a parent and it's so stressful and you lose your confidence too. When everyone's saying 'No' to you, you start to lose confidence that you're doing the right thing. I think that's something you get over the years, a bit more confidence, or stronger in saying what you want, more assertive I suppose.

He's mainstreamed. I had to fight for it because the children they've had at school previous to Joseph haven't had as severe a disability as Joseph and they thought he was a bit too hard. He started doing half days. Our understanding was that after a time for him to settle in, the hours would be extended. When we wanted to extend the time, all they said was, 'We don't think he's ready and we're not ready.' But the Special Education Services were saying, 'We've got the teacher aide hours for you.' So we had a big meeting with Intellectually Handicapped Children (IHC) advocates and let the principal and teachers know kindly but firmly about Joseph's legal right to be at school full time and all of a sudden they said he should go for a full day.

It's going really well.

MOTHER OF KEVIN: 30 YEARS

Kevin really thrived at the local secondary school. Although he never really acquired any real friends there, the kids tolerated him. It was good for them as well as for him because they could really see somebody who wasn't handicapped in as much that he didn't walk with a limp, or had a funny face, or any physical or obvious disability. He was just different. They accepted it very well and of course that helped him because he didn't stick out like a sore thumb amongst the other children. He really spent the best years of his life, with the least problems, when he was at the secondary college. He was in a disciplined society and it was a very disciplined school compared with other schools. But it was that sort of environment that he needed and it really worked very well. He did very well because he actually sat School Certificate exams. But he only passed in mathematics and of course mathematics is the thing that's mechanical. He didn't really come close with anything else, least of all English, but mathematics he passed.

MOTHER OF JOSEPH: 7 YEARS

It's hard. You just have to keep fighting as you go along. There are still teachers in the school that you'd like to punch their lights out. It's quite difficult but you have to get alongside them because you need to. I think it takes mainstream schools a long time to accept, 'Yes, they have this responsibility.' They do not accept that Joseph is a boy who is seven, therefore he has a right to be at school all day. Even now it's like they're doing us a big favour. Every time something goes wrong they have to tell you about it and how terrible it was and make you feel as though you should be apologizing a thousand times. Whereas with a normal child, if that happened, it would be dealt with in the school system a lot of the time.

It's the same with resources and funding. When it comes to Joseph they say, 'We can't do this, he'll have to stay at home.' Little things like a relieving teacher. One of their excuses for not letting him go to school for longer was the teacher in the new entrant class had so many children coming through. Their rationale was Joseph was less important than the normal children and was better off staying at home. Probably while there's still Special Schools around it'll be like that. It's not really their responsibility because there's always that option. Teachers have said to me, 'There's a really good Special School in the town nearby. Joseph would be much better off there.' We don't live in that town and he's doing fine at school.

MOTHER OF PETER: 17 YEARS

Most people's hang-ups about Peter are through ignorance. The things they say to you like, 'What's your son's life expectancy?' I've had that one for years. It's so hurtful. You say to yourself, 'Don't retaliate, they're just ignorant.' Sometimes I turn around and say, 'What's your child's life expectancy?' and they say, 'Well, I thought it might be different because…' It's amazing, isn't it? I guess it's up to us to change that.

MOTHER OF JOSEPH: 7 YEARS

We've got a different teacher aide, which has really helped. At the same time as extending his hours, the first teacher aide resigned because she found working with Joseph too stressful. A lady who had been doing IHC home help and shared care for us offered to be his teacher aide. She sees him just about more than I see him really. But she's got the personality to cope with it. She's not a trained teacher, but she and Joseph just get on the same wavelength and nothing fazes her. She doesn't get angry with him, and she doesn't feel apologetic about him or feel intimidated by the rest of the school when they look at her as if to say, 'Sort that kid out.' She just holds her ground. That's worked out because she doesn't get wound up, then Joseph doesn't get wound up and it doesn't spiral downward. He's really part of the school and he's part of the community. He's being an everyday kid. There's things he does differently and he has his own peculiarities, but he's out there doing stuff.

MOTHER OF PETER: 17 YEARS

Peter still gets very upset going into supermarkets. He'll just stand there with his hands over his face and he won't move and people are pushing their carts around him. When I take Peter to tennis they look at him strangely, like if I sit next to him you may get some disease or something. People can't understand why he does strange things and won't speak. When he was little, he'd make some funny noise and people would stare. It didn't worry my other son and me. His brother would just stare back at these people. It's easier too when you're with someone. You can have a laugh about it later. For years that's how you get through it by having a sense of humour and laughing about all the crazy things that's happened. But sometimes they're not funny. I've always laughed and sometimes my husband has told me off and said, 'That's not funny,' but you have to laugh.

A lot of things he's done over the years were funny. Like we'd walk into a restaurant and as we were walking past a table he'd grab someone's drink and start drinking it, or he'd reach out and grab the chips off the fork as they're about to go into the person's mouth and the person would be left there with their mouth open.

FAMILY OF JOHN: 8 YEARS

Mother: You have to become very thick-skinned so that you don't get embarrassed. Sometimes you just have to remove him as quickly as you can. But if he senses that, he yells even louder. You have to entice him into something else, often it's food, just to get him to leave.

But he can be very, very good. He can be perfect and it just takes something and he switches. It usually is associated with something that he's fanatical about.

The thing with John is that he has these different moods and depending what mood he's in, depends on what he's like. It's like living with different people really.

Sister: 10 years: In plazas, John's thrown this real wobbly and he's lain on the floor and Mum's tried unsuccessfully to pick him up. People don't know that he's handicapped. People think he's just normal and being really naughty and they'll come up to him and yell and that just makes it worse. But Mum's got these cards now (explaining about autism) and she hands them out to people.

Mother: Or the time in McDonald's, where he threw a wobbly in the middle of the restaurant. We were more concerned with evacuating than educating the staring public. He had a sore bottom and he told everyone. He wanted to take his trousers off, 'Why can't I take my trousers off, why can't I take my trousers off?' When he gets like that, you just have to leave as quickly as you can.

MOTHER OF KEVIN: 30 YEARS

His behaviour was pretty diabolical. I have been thrown out of every supermarket in the area. I was asked to 'Get off at the next station' on the trains. I was actually physically removed a couple of times from Woolworths in town. I was taken by the arm and asked to 'Remove that child' because I didn't know 'how to control that child' and I must have been a 'pretty disgusting parent'.

MOTHER OF JOSEPH: 7 YEARS

I find it hard that the general public don't know about autism. I say 'Joseph has autism' and they just look at me. Then I say, 'Joseph is intellectually handicapped.' 'Well, he doesn't look IH (intellectually handicapped),' they say, 'You should just give him a good smack. This lovely looking little boy needs a bit of discipline.' That's what I find so hard. Just because it's not a common thing and because he looks so normal and he is a nice-looking little boy, when he behaves so inappropriately people just look at you with this frown on their face and you just have to walk off.

MOTHER OF PETER: 17 YEARS

Peter had operations on his feet. He was born with flat feet. It was obviously painful. He would just sit down on the road in the middle of wherever he was. We were living in Singapore at the time. We went to this professor who was an authority on feet for the whole of South East Asia at the time. He was in the operating theatre for about six or seven hours. I was just about beside myself and no-one would tell me anything that was going on. It was a very painful operation whereas he made out it was a more minor thing. Peter was in agony. I remember one day, the first day when he first went into hospital, they said, 'Your son won't speak to us,' and I said, 'No, he's handicapped', because I thought they wouldn't understand autistic and they said, 'Yes, but why didn't he speak to us?' So I said, 'Handicap, no speak' and they said, 'He looks so normal.' He was about ten years of age at this time and they couldn't understand why he wouldn't speak to them. Even though he wouldn't speak, they still expected him to understand everything they did and said to him and he was absolutely amazing. I think he only cried once and I thought it would turn him right off me, that he would associate me with the pain, that I had done it to him. That was my worst fear and that didn't happen. He actually grabbed my hand and held on to me. He just wanted me there, just wouldn't let go. He made me sit there and I sat there for about a week, day and night. I wouldn't leave him.

PARENTS OF JENNY: 2 YEARS

Father: Shopping, I go to the supermarket first. I have all these things that I have to do and by the time we're finished at the supermarket, I give up. At first I found it even worse because I thought everyone was looking at her, talking about her. My wife has got a lot thicker-skinned now. I was shocking at first.

Mother: She loves going out but she's naughty. Jenny doesn't know she's being naughty when she's out. She pulls things off shelves. Things that are funny to her just aren't to me. I've had a few comments, usually from older people, who really have no patience with children. One woman said, 'Tell your daughter to stop screaming.' (She has a high-pitched squeal and because a supermarket is so big and open, it echoes.) I said, 'I can't. She doesn't understand.' This was before I found out about her being autistic. And then she said, 'Give her a hiding then.' I turned around and said, 'Excuse me, how dare you.' She was quite stunned. She didn't say anything to me after that, but I was quite upset when I got home.

FAMILY OF DAVID: 8 YEARS

Mother: I remember walking around the supermarket with him and people giving me a wide berth. Even though you had this lovely looking child, he would be doing something unusual. He'd just run up and down the supermarket, or roll along. He would also get on the boots and bonnets of the cars outside and of course the people didn't like that. The public didn't really seem to be very knowledgeable about autism when David was little, but I feel they are a bit more so. I used to say to people when David was doing something strange, 'He's autistic' and they'd say, 'Oh, like Rain Man.' They would immediately know and I wouldn't have to explain. Even though he was nothing like him, at least it provided some understanding.

The other parents' attitudes were the hardest thing about having a child with autism. I used to see these parents standing there, staring and often criticizing. That was really hard.

PARENTS OF ALEX: 7 YEARS

Father: Even though Alex is obsessive about going to the supermarket, there are few situations that arise in the supermarket where her behaviour is other than exemplary.

Mother: Except when they change the floor polish.

Father: There are occasions when she'll lie on the floor, or hug the supervisor, but generally they wouldn't know there had been a special needs child through there. Her behaviour is generally pretty good.

Mother: They did have a change of floor polish once though, and she launched herself across the lino and sniffed deeply which most children don't do. But she got over that.

The supermarket behaviour started way back when Alex was first diagnosed. That was one of the first things I did as a parent in the community. We called it our 'public education day' and we started out at the supermarket.

I figured out that if I had to leave a trolley of food because of Alex's inappropriate behaviour, I was actually providing employment for someone to stack them back on the shelf. And that no-one ever died of embarrassment though you could come damn close to it. It took a year. I would get cash and go straight to the cake section. Alex would choose one thing, then we would go straight back out through the 'cash' checkout. To begin with she could only tolerate being in the supermarket for five or six minutes. We'd get to the end of a month and we'd get to the end of one aisle. By the end of the year, we could go around the whole supermarket. But it took a year and it took courage.

PARENTS OF JENNY: 2 YEARS

Mother: It's so difficult too, because a little child in a wheel-chair or a child with Down Syndrome has a visible disability, which autism isn't. In fact, most autistic kids are very beautiful children. You say, 'My child's autistic,' and people will either give a 'Oh yes,' as if they know, or 'Oh, just like Rain Man.'

I've had a few people ask, 'What is autism?' But not many. They just look at you as if you're strange.

PARENTS OF ALEX: 7 YEARS

Mother: Then we got the whole library routine off pat. She now marches over, sometimes forgetting her card, and the librarian stands there staring at her until I rescue both of them. Over the past few months I have stood back. But Alex tends to throw the books and the card at the librarian. And then she tends to walk away and leave the card behind. But I'm still at the stage where I prompt her to pick up her card. I really must write something down for the librarian and explain Alex's difficulties.

At the end of the term she got really tired and she got muddled. The librarians manage with dignity. I think they must be used to dealing with a huge range of human personalities in those libraries and Alex is just one at the other end of the continuum. That's also taken a year. Prior to that, libraries were places you whipped in and out of. Alex has been told off by the supervisor at the swimming pool. She looks normal, they think she's normal and so they expect normal, appropriate behaviour from her. Adults can get quite confused. Generally I have the energy to explain about autism if I have to. These days I don't tend to. But in the early days if I didn't have the emotional energy, sometimes I would just lie and say she was deaf. There are still times when we go out socially, that I don't make eye contact with anybody because then I would know if they were staring at us or not. I can still feel embarrassed by her behaviour.

MOTHER OF PETER: 17 YEARS

I met a great woman who had a child with Down Syndrome and she'd joined the Down Syndrome Association. She said to me once, 'It's much harder for you than it is for me. My daughter looks as if she has Down Syndrome. Everyone knows she is disabled. They don't bother staring any more because they know. Whereas Peter looks so normal and people stare all the time wondering why he's behaving that way.' She helped me a lot.

PARENTS OF ELEANOR: 7 YEARS

Father: Autism also affects things out of the home. It affects my job, because considering positions in other parts of the country is just out of the question. You've built up relation-ships with professionals, schools, that you really can't afford to sacrifice. The thought of moving her out of this house is unrealistic. We've got neighbours who understand her and will just return things when she throws them over the fence. Another neighbour will leave a little pile of objects in the garage when she walks past. That's a marvellous rapport we've built up. They are very sympathetic. She's not allowed to scream in the garden. If she's being excessive, she comes straight inside. We try to be considerate.

Mother: One of our neighbours used to leave her light on in the living room and not draw the curtains. When we just had wire fence down the back she used to notice that Eleanor would be out in the garden at twilight and would watch the light. She loved the light so the neighbour used to keep the curtains open, which was so sweet of her.

FAMILY OF DAVID: 8 YEARS

Grandparents: It has been very interesting and has given us a better understanding of children. We were in the supermarket the other day and a child was screaming and screaming. People would say, 'The child deserves a spanking.' But how do we know it wasn't a child with problems? You're not so quick to condemn like you usually are.

PARENTS OF RICHARD: 11 YEARS

Father: When we first found out that Richard was autistic, I made up my mind I would never leave this area. It's too valuable for him. He's got all his friends and acquaintances who just say, 'hello'. They are all important to him. He knows more people than the average kid. He's got a good memory and he's familiar with a great number of people.

Richard is a well-recognized figure in the community. Go down to the supermarket and there's always someone who knows Richard. They don't know me but they know Richard. 'Who's that old guy with Richard?' He's got a really good memory but he tends to be very selective with it. He only remembers people who are nice to him.

Over the last two years he's been invited to quite a few birthday parties. He's enjoyed those. He looks forward to the parties now and he shows an interest in everybody there, and the other kids like that.

FAMILY OF JOHN: 8 YEARS

Father: We've enrolled John in Cubs. That seems to work really well because it's a very small group of people. There are only 13 or 14 boys, a small enough group to get to know John quite intimately, and in a controlled environment. There was initially a bit of resistance from some of the kids. They were teasing John and it took a couple of sessions with them by the leader of the group who explained John's situation and why he was as he was. Now they're really good.

We went to a Cub camp. I took him up and I went fully expecting to share a tent with him but one of the other boys wanted to share a tent with John and so he was accepted into the group. I was quite surprised.

Sister: There's a deaf boy at Cubs and he's really good with John. He's probably the best one there. He invites John to do things and it's good that he talks quite loudly and clearly because John needs that sort of talk. If you mumble at him he won't pay any attention. It's like he can't be bothered with the fuss of, 'What did you say?' He won't say it. If he hasn't heard it, he will ignore it. You have to speak clearly to get through to him sometimes.

This girl from up the road, she comes often. One time we took John to the swimming pool and these boys were there and they were teasing him and she told them off. She yelled at them and really stuck up for him. It was really good.

MOTHER OF JOSEPH: 7 YEARS

Joseph's classmates are going to grow up to be adults that don't have a problem with handicapped people basically. They haven't got the fear that all of us have got because we didn't have handicapped people in schools. So when we see one as an adult we think, 'What do we do? If I say hello he might make a funny noise.' Whereas they just say, 'Hi Joseph.' They've been saying it since he was five and they will continue doing it and it won't faze them. They'll be 'autistically' aware and I just think that's so important as a parent, that society has a good attitude towards Joseph. It's part of my job to educate people in a nice way, not a pushy way, because people can get a bit like, 'This is my son's right.' So people out of sheer fear go along with it. I want it to be a positive thing. Joseph is their friend. He had a party and they all came and they invited him to their parties. It's really good.

MOTHER OF KEVIN: 30 YEARS

He has just moved from the first house that he went to. It's now the highest level house that he can live in and hopefully he will be able to stay there, maybe for years. I hope so because he's in with three other men who are in exactly the same situation. They're not autistic. They are people who have obviously had traumatic things happen in their lives, maybe through illness, maybe through accidents. But he has settled in. He didn't want to make the move and he actually refused several times. His caregivers at the other house said that they really felt he was ready and I said, 'I will help you talk him into it.' And he settled. I just couldn't believe it. That he could've literally settled overnight. And he really does like it and now he's just started to talk about when I go home. So he realizes, he knows this is home in as much as this is where mother lives, but that is where he's got his little nest.

CHAPTER 4

'You can't try and rush them'

As we are increasingly aware, children with autism perceive things differently. They learn differently and in most cases require a very different method of teaching from other children. But there is no 'typical' autistic child. There is no 'one size fits all' way to teach them. They learn in their own way and at their own pace. As with all children, they have their own personalities, their own interests, strengths and fears. Sometimes we just have to be patient to observe the strategies they use to learn, before teaching them our way.

FAMILY OF JOHN: 8 YEARS

Mother: John is doing things now, that when he was a preschooler I wouldn't have believed, like that when he was eight he could read. He's reading journals. He's bringing home quite big readers. I remember the first time I saw him write 'John', I was stunned.

Sister: 10 years: The first time he wrote 'John' we were in the car. Me and my little sister had been writing on the window because it was frosted up that morning. Then John was sitting by the door and he just wrote on the window, wrote it out, 'John'.

Mother: That was staggering. He was five and a half then. I would never have believed that he could have done that. The whole way that he's learnt to read and to write too has come down to patterns. John knows the patterns of the word and recognizes the whole word and so when he approaches a word that he doesn't know, he can get quite cross. What they're working on now, and actually it is starting to work, is the sounding out, the initial sounds and consonants, which he is learning too as a rote thing. He has a very good memory so he can learn to approach words from recognizing the initial sounds too. But that certainly isn't how he has learnt to read. He's learnt from memorizing the whole pattern of the word and he either knows it or he doesn't.

'Photo' made him really angry, which in itself shows that he was looking at the initial sound; it should be 'f'. That was quite recently. Because in his mind he was right. The same too with adding. If he has decided that 2 + 3 is 6, then it is. He is right. He used to get quite worked up because he will have decided something and you can't actually talk him through something like that, though he is getting the hang of adding and using concrete things. He's coming on quite well.

MOTHER OF JOSEPH: 7 YEARS

He's done quite well on the computer. He's concentrated really well which is unusual for Joseph, because up till now anything academic and he's just not there. He has started to do maths on the whiteboard. His teacher aide writes the question and then gives him four different solutions and he has to rub out the answer he thinks is correct. He gets it right which is really good. He can't write. He has trouble getting his fingers to hold the pen. We are looking into getting him his own computer. So I'm really pleased about that.

PARENTS OF ALEX: 7 YEARS

Father: She picked up this book this evening. First time I have ever seen her do it. She opened the pages and she was signing as she read through it. She was signing the pictures, particularly the last three pages. I think she's reading inside her head.

MOTHER OF MICHAEL: 4 YEARS

It wasn't until he didn't learn to talk that I became concerned. All the other behaviours could be explained away. Even his music teacher said to me, 'Oh, don't worry about that. My son didn't start to talk until he was five years old and there's nothing wrong with him.' And other things like the fixation with 'Thomas the Tank Engine'. I saw other children have exactly the same fixation with Thomas and do exactly the same things as Michael did with videos. So to a large extent I didn't worry too much. Again his lack of play with toys.

He had some wonderful toys that he never used, still hasn't used. He's got dump trucks that are as good as the day they were bought. But again I found other women saying to me that they had the same trouble with their children. That they had a room full of toys they wouldn't play with.

Little things, like the fact that he wouldn't know what to do with a birthday present if it fell on his head, worried me. He didn't know that he was supposed to open it. He didn't know that he was supposed to blow out the birthday candles on the cake and I knew other children were able to do this. That was when I started wondering what was wrong. I felt I was floundering around for information. I didn't know the first step of where to go and find out what was wrong with him. That was what I found hard; very hard.

MOTHER OF PETER: 17 YEARS

I remember one day when he was at preschool and I was sitting there looking at the kids. Some of them were quite badly handicapped, quite physically handicapped as well, and yet Peter stood out, different to all of them. He was the one that looked so normal and so lovely looking. Yet I thought that there was something really different; he's different to all of them. He's worse than all of them because he doesn't have any eye contact. These kids that were so crippled, they could still look at you. They couldn't even get food in their mouth but they could look at you. Peter didn't.

Someone put the word autism into my head when he was about two years old. I don't even know where it came from. I raced down to the library and got all the books out on autism. There weren't many around but I thought, 'Yes, that's definitely him.'

When he was four, we came up to the city to get his hearing tested because they thought he was deaf. We discovered that there was nothing wrong with his hearing, so that reinforced it for me that he must be autistic.

FAMILY OF DAVID: 8 YEARS

Mother: David's development was very slow. He didn't develop like a normal baby, especially his speech and behaviour, but he was physically quick in everything. When walking, he was very balanced. He was capable of walking along narrow rails and climbing. He was very agile. There was no eye contact at all early on. He never really had it. It's the other way now.

Grandfather: The way his mother persisted on getting eye contact and getting through David's barrier is the reason he has improved so dramatically.

Mother: I was reading in a magazine about the actor from M.A.S.H. who has an autistic son. He was being interviewed and he described his son and I thought, 'That sounds like David.' So I went to the library and got all these books out. Five of the six were incredibly depressing and basically said you might as well give up hope and stick him in an institution. They were all like that except one written by 'Kaufmann'. I just went about copying what she did with her son because it was the only positive approach. I didn't work as long hours as she did. I didn't have the time to do it. We just did two or three hours a day. We never went along with confrontation. Every book was all overseas, mostly American. One of the books had a list of autistic features at the back and we could tick every one.

That's when I realized definitely that he was autistic. Also, mothers know. It was a real relief to find out that it wasn't just isolated behavioural problems. It was one thing and I could deal with that.

FAMILY OF JOHN: 8 YEARS

Mother: Toileting has been a long-term issue. At eight he started taking himself to the toilet. It's taken eight years. He still wears nappies to bed. I actually went for two years putting him to bed without nappies and getting him up in the night and taking him to the toilet and I got sick of it. He's promised when he turns nine, he'll stop wearing nappies. It was quite confusing for him because nappies are for babies and, 'Why do I wear nappies?' So we said, 'You can stop wearing nappies when you stop wetting the bed. When are you going to stop going wees in the bed, John?' And he said, 'When I'm nine.' He turns nine next May so we'll see if he's got enough control to deliver on his promise. During the day now he hasn't wet his pants for weeks, which is wonderful. I used to send half a dozen changes to school and they came back all wet. But he's pretty good. Up until a month ago he was still wetting his pants once a week at least. His toileting was entirely controlled by us but now he's actually saying he wants to go to the toilet and that's a major breakthrough. We've done lots of washing over the years. It's a bit like his food. You can't bribe him, he has to be ready. We've gone through getting cross with him and it didn't work. He just didn't have the control or the desire to go even and that's a long battle. You can't try and rush them or train them ahead. At most times it comes down to when they're ready. With John, he was ready a lot later.

Autism has been around a long time but it's a modern phenomenon that's still not fully understood.

FAMILY OF DAVID: 8 YEARS

Mother: We got him off his obsession with power poles using the bucket of Lego when he was three. I used to sit down with him and make power poles out of the Lego. We did that for a long time; we all made power poles. Then a few weeks later, I built a wall and he was quite interested in that wall and thought that was pretty good. He still didn't build it but he kept looking at it. Then one night he just built this wall himself and after that he was just away, building. He was mad on building things with Lego and wooden blocks. He also loved the sandpit. He built things and smashed things. He used to love the feel of wheat. We had wheat growing in the garden. Once we found something that he was interested in, we would accept what he did, then gradually change it. We couldn't force the change though.

PARENTS OF RICHARD: 11 YEARS

Father: A few years ago, Richard used to ignore me, so I began to tease him. You could see him coming out of his shell and he would respond and be a bit annoyed with me and it was good. I used to do that quite often as a tool to get him to respond and I do it a bit now.

The hardest thing is continually having to find new things for him, because I reckon he could still be doing better than he is. If you could just find out what he is interested in. I would like to see a new passion that would tax him mentally and I feel as though that would bring him out. An interest that he was dead keen on. I think that would be invaluable, but to find that...

One thing he seems to have a rapport with is art. He seems to have a flair for it. He certainly doesn't inherit it. Maybe next year we should enrol him in art classes after school.

FAMILY OF DAVID: 8 YEARS

Mother: He is excellent at making things out of Lego. He used to be extremely symmetrical. If he had so many yellow on one side, there had to be exactly the same on the other side. He is not so symmetrical now. He is very realistic. He will now make a tyrannosaurus and working 'technic' models without plans.

He's also very good at drawing. You ask him to draw a face and he draws a profile. We really encourage his drawing. He drew dinosaurs for a while but he'll draw all sorts now.

FAMILY OF JOHN: 8 YEARS

Mother: We really feel that he's benefited a lot from the special needs programme because of the precision, the way it has been targeted to his needs. I think that if we decided that we were just going to mainstream him from the start, I think we would have regretted it. I don't think he'd be reading as well as he is. In fact, when he had the combination of the Special School and the regular school, I used to feel that his actual learning, in terms of academic learning like reading and understanding mathematical things, was happening at the Special School and he was just using it at the regular school, because the way that they teach isn't the way that he learns. They teach to the average and, particularly with reading, so much is just expected to be picked up. This has worked with our other two children because they're quite bright but John doesn't just pick up anything like that. He's had to be taught in a very different way, with cards, activities using words over and over, lots of repetition. His actual reading now is not that far behind some of the other children. But the whole approach to teaching it has been completely different. It's been more akin to a training programme. That's even true for some things that aren't academic, such as social behaviour. Regular children tend to pick it up, it tends to rub off. It doesn't rub off on John. We have to train him and we're going to have to keep training him as to what's appropriate where. Hopefully the aim is to have one of the satellite classes in our local area. That would be the ideal.

MOTHER OF JOSEPH: 7 YEARS

They've got a special needs room they've built. The deputy principal organized this. There's four little classrooms which is good because Joseph does find being in the class all the time a bit much. It's not in his best interest to be in class all the time. He can go to his little room where he and his teacher have all their resources, like their music. It's good. It's a bit of a balance. You have to be realistic. There's some things about the mainstream system that just don't suit Joseph, that are too difficult for him.

FAMILY OF DAVID: 8 YEARS

Mother: Finding things that he was interested in was a key, and getting him into speech therapy early. We were told by the specialist psychiatrist who first diagnosed David at three and a half, that his success in life would ultimately depend on his IQ (intelligence quotient) and his language capabilities. We therefore felt that speech therapy was essential, even though our GP (general practitioner) was reluctant to refer us at such an early age. He was 20 months old when therapy started with strategies to get that first sound. We'd try to get him to say sounds and he'd be trying so hard and he would say something that was nothing like it at all. Like 'Mummy' he would say 'barble'. He'd watch when you said it, then he'd come out with 'barble'. You'd go to the supermarket and you'd hear his voice calling out, 'barble, barble' and it was David calling 'Mum'. He was four and a half when he first started calling me 'Mum'. Mind you, his first word was 'daisy'. If he could say 'daisy' he should be able to say these other things, but no.

PARENTS OF RICHARD: 11 YEARS

Mother: The school has the right attitude to helping children like Richard and because of that he's gone ahead in leaps and bounds.

Mainstreaming is good, but you really need the right school that's sympathetic to helping children like Richard. I can't speak highly enough of what the school has done for him. It's just an ordinary school. It's not a school that caters for special needs. It has special needs funding allocated. It's really great.

Mainstreaming with all those other children has spurred him on a bit. He goes to school camps. The first school camp really made a difference to his language. On the Friday of the camp he was actually chatting to everybody. It was obvious after an intense four or five days. On the Friday the children were coming up and saying, 'Richard's been talking to us.' They were so excited about it. A lot of them who were older and from different parts of the school didn't know Richard talked at all.

Just before the holidays he wrote his first story with imagination and it was: *A Trip to the City: One day I went on a bus to the city. I was going to the movies. The bus crashed into the traffic lights. A lady banged her head and she fell out of the bus. She went to the doctor. A man fixed the bus and the bus went to the city.'* But it's something which he hasn't experienced.

FAMILY OF DAVID: 8 YEARS

Mother: He used to sing the National Anthem when he was 14 months old. He did funny things. I remember one day he sat up in the bath and he was about one and a half and he'd never spoken. He'd only said that one word 'daisy' and he said, 'To be or not to be, that is the question.' I don't know where he got that from and I never heard it again. I thought I was hearing things. It's all going in, no doubt about that. It was just trying to get it out.

David now speaks very well and has done since the age of about six and a half. His intonation is excellent and appropriate. This is a direct result of speech therapy techniques used intensively at the speech clinic, school and at home, mostly accompanied by playing with David and getting him interested in whatever the subject of the play was. Once echolalia and pronoun reversal stopped, his language just took off like a bomb. (Echolalia is the immediate or delayed echoing or exact repetition of a word or complete phrase.)

MOTHER OF JOSEPH: 7 YEARS

We use gentle teaching. It does work with Joseph. His teacher aide is even better at it than me. Sometimes I think she's a bit over the top but you need to be, otherwise you wouldn't last the distance. She believes so much in Joseph and his ability. She thinks he's very clever and he actually does some clever things for her because she tells him she knows he can do it. I think that's very important. I think there's more up there than we give him credit for. You have to be careful what you say around him, because sometimes he doesn't understand what you say but you can say the same thing another time and he'll understand it as clear as day. It is important to believe in him.

MOTHER OF MICHAEL: 4 YEARS

He is quite aware that the other children can talk and he can't. He gets so much joy and pleasure out of being able to say a word, you wouldn't believe. He lies there in bed in the mornings and I say, 'How about some words' and he goes 'my, my, my, mum, mum, mum,' and then he tries really hard to get his mouth into the right shape to say 'your'. He goes 'yyyy', really thinks about it for about ten seconds or more, 'yyyour', and then he goes 'your' and he's so pleased with himself. We clap and he's just thrilled. He is tickled to bits to be able to say a word. He's decided on this word. I think he knows what it means. But he has decided to start practising it and doing it. He's just so thrilled to be able to say one word.

MOTHER OF JOSEPH: 7 YEARS

I really have no idea what he'll be like. I see how he is now is how he will be when he's grown up. It's not to say I just let him 'vege' around. He keeps being taught. He'll match objects and colours but it doesn't interest him much, that's the problem. I think he could do it really easily but he just doesn't have the motivation. If there's something else that really motivates him, like trying to get a can of something really yummy, he'll climb up into the cupboards and he will work on it for ages and ages. But that's the basic problem. He finds colouring in just totally boring. He hates it. It's not because he can't colour in, he can colour in fine. He's got the fine motor skills but he doesn't want to colour in.

FAMILY OF DAVID: 8 YEARS

Mother: At school he's in groups now for reading, writing and maths and has been for some months. We had to wean him off the one-to-one attention, otherwise he becomes dependent and won't do things without assistance. He's good in groups and is beginning to work as an independent member of the class. Reading and maths are at his age level. Written language is imaginative and shows good vocabulary but he tends to forget about punctuation.

David is very visual and learns visually. He is now reading journals just a little below his age level. He doesn't like fairy stories. He hates them. He has to have real life.

PARENTS OF RICHARD: 11 YEARS

Father: Richard is 11 years old now. He's been speaking clearly and with meaning for about two years. His reading and writing are improving. He's able to spell out loud now too. He seemed to change after he had the 'sensory integration' when he was nine (a programme designed to assist the child's brain to efficiently process and organize sensory messages such as touch; movement; sight; sounds; smell; taste that they receive from their own body and from the world around them). He went from July to December once a week and then in the third term he went horseriding as well. That whole intensity of the physical side seems to have unravelled something somewhere. Since then he has started to speak.

Before then he'd make choices with food but he didn't speak in sentences. And the pronouns have only come this year. He will now say 'I' instead of 'Richard'. He used to talk about himself as though he were a different person, but now he's saying 'I'. That was a major breakthrough. Realistically, it's very difficult to keep talking to someone who never answers you.

He's stopped talking to himself quite as much too. At night when he lies in bed, he doesn't talk and make the silly noises he used to make. When he woke up in the mornings he used to squeal and make silly noises. He's stopped echoing what you say and will now answer you. He uses 'yes' and 'no' usually appropriately, whereas one time he used to say 'yes' just to get rid of you. Sometimes he still does but he promptly corrects himself. He realizes I'm not going to accept his answer.

MOTHER OF JOSEPH: 7 YEARS

With Joseph they say 'Draw a circle.' How many years do you have to be drawing circles? That's half the problem in some areas. He doesn't move on. So they keep doing the same stuff and he just gets totally bored. They do these tests to measure his IQ, it's very depressing. They say, 'Will he do this?' And I'll say, 'No, but he can do it.' He did it when he was two and half or three but he hasn't been able to move on to the next step in it. So he's still having to do the same thing and he's getting bored with it. That's the big problem with Joseph. He's still on drawing circles, he hasn't moved on to drawing 'people'. Like the children with autism who know their alphabet brilliantly at two years of age and can't move on to putting the letters together to make words. The alphabet to them is not the same as the alphabet to us. It's just a pattern, a routine, a system, all those lovely things they like. It's not an alphabet, it's not what makes words, it's not communication. It's very difficult to grasp all of that.

Joseph loves music, he's a very good dancer. He'll listen to music. He gets a lot of enjoyment out of listening to music but once again he hasn't done anything musical. But he's happy with his music so that's fine with us. It's nice to see him happy and appreciating something. One of his senses has been stimulated.

MOTHER OF KEVIN: 30 YEARS

He went in to work, got a job, just as a factory worker, a process worker. Now, he was fine to start with but he became bored. He'd gone up to a certain point, to a potential, and really he could've gone a lot further but there was nothing that he really fitted into. I tried getting him down to have a computer course which was fine as far as his skills on a keyboard go. He can type faster than I can. He's got phenomenal speed and accuracy on the keyboard and all fingers as though he'd learnt. But when it came to the computer side, it might be easier now, but of course now it would be motivating him into learning because he has this awful mindset now that he can't do these things. But he found in the course, in the formal training sort of session, that all the jargon was just beyond him. Ordinary everyday words took long enough to get the handle on, so to be able to use it in computer jargon was just way beyond him. So he sort of gave up, which was a shame. It's a pity there isn't a form of learning set-up for people with disabilities that would give them the skills, because they seem to have it there. It's just finding the right way of feeding it to them so they take it on board and know how to use it. But, however, that's yet another hurdle I suppose, that will probably be overcome over a period of years.

FAMILY OF DAVID: 8 YEARS

Mother: We weren't sure whether he would have to go to a Special School and that was a big worry. I really believed he would have to. He wasn't doing what he was told at kindergarten and he wasn't participating in the activities. We thought Special School definitely. Then they extended his time at kindergarten for six months and when he was five and a half, we went looking at the schools.

The psychologist said the best thing for him would be a special class attached to a normal school and then mainstream him for different subjects. But when the teachers of the school came to have a look at him, they didn't feel he was really suitable for the special class, so they said, 'Let's give him a go in the mainstream.' We've been very lucky with all the people we've had dealings with, excellent teacher aides, good speech therapists and itinerant teachers as well as a very positive principal. David has gone ahead at school and we've just had a meeting where they are going to withdraw all the support, so we'll see what happens.

CHAPTER 5

'We've been able to gradually expand his environment'

In order to assist their child to cope with the demands of everyday life and the expectations of society, parents often devise some original techniques in order to teach the necessary skills. The children need to learn how to cope with change, to learn appropriate behaviour, manage stress and to accept that life is not always on their terms. They also need to learn the rules essential to keep themselves healthy and safe.

MOTHER OF KEVIN: 30 YEARS

I started all those years ago what I call the 'today book'. Now I believe it's quite common practice. I 'nailed' him down in the bed at night and I would have a big pad of paper. I can't draw to save my soul, but I used to do pin men and I would make him look at me. Over a period of time I did get some eye contact with him and so I would make him look at me and I would say, 'We're going to talk about what we've done' and I would head up 'today'. I would draw me on a little pin with a skirt and he would look at the pictures so that it became, like a lot of things with autistic children, a routine. It was something that he was programmed for, so that he would almost expect 'today' every evening. But it did work, because he started to acquire a degree of recall which showed that there must have been something there. It certainly helped to get some foundation for him to recall things and go over and over and over the little things like, 'Today we get out of bed and wash our hands and face.' That went on every day on the same thing so that he took it for granted that that's how life ticked over. I did that right up until he was nine or ten.

PARENTS OF ALEX: 7 YEARS

Mother: Alex generally doesn't react badly to a change of routine. But that was early training. In the early days she could have become quite obsessive in the route that we took from kindergarten to home. Every so often I'd change it. I used to change it just a little bit, nothing major but just enough to stop the obsession becoming overpowering. Because our kiddies with autism can really rule the roost and sometimes cause a major loss of parental control in families. Very, very strong-willed children that can make life quite hellish for the whole family.

MOTHER OF MICHAEL: 4 YEARS

I took him for his two-year check and the nurse said, 'He really should have some words by now. Let's take him off to speech therapy.' He would have been about two years and three months then. I took him to see the therapist and Michael got hysterical, because it was a new environment. It was a small room and I think he thought I was going to leave him at another child care centre as I had done in the past. Whenever I had attempted to work, I had to leave him at child care centres and it was the biggest nightmare of my life. I could hear this screaming mess. He could not be left anywhere. The only place he could be left was with my mother and I couldn't leave him with my mother all the time. It wasn't fair on her.

FAMILY OF JOHN: 8 YEARS

Mother: Dealing with John's anger is a major thing. It's hard. If he didn't have such an explosive temper, he'd be a lot of fun. But when he loses his temper, he's really loud. That's the thing with John in public places. It doesn't matter where he is, he doesn't give a damn. Telling him to be quiet doesn't do anything. He doesn't have the social awareness.

FAMILY OF DAVID: 8 YEARS

Mother: When we were in the supermarket, if they made an announcement, David would scream. However, if the phone rang beside him, he appeared not to hear it. I remember when he was nine months old, I dropped all the pots and pans out of the cupboard. He never moved, he never blinked, he didn't do anything. Yet other things he would hear.

FAMILY OF JOHN: 8 YEARS

Father: He can't help talking to himself. Some of his best conversations are with himself. He's more lucid with himself than with other people.

Mother: It's like he's thinking out loud. He punishes himself. Like if he hits someone. That's been a major thing, hitting.

He goes to his room and he sits on the chair and you put the timer on. He's allowed off the chair when the timer goes. If he hits himself, he'll punish himself. He'll take himself to his room, and tell himself off and put the timer on.

Sister: When Mum takes him in there, she puts the timer on for a couple of minutes. Then John will go in there and put it on for half an hour. And he'll sit there. He has before put it on to half an hour and I've gone in there and changed it. But if we didn't change it he'd be prepared to sit there for half an hour.

FAMILY OF DAVID: 8 YEARS

Mother: I see autism as being an emotional dysfunction, impaired reality. David seemed to not be affected by anything emotional. Like something sad. But now he's the absolute opposite. He is more emotional than any other child I know. Looking at the expressions on the faces of the people he has drawn, I know he is feeling very strong emotions but he is trying to hide them. One day when Bruce Springsteen's song 'Streets of Philadelphia' was on the radio, he asked me what it was about. I told him and he understood. That night he couldn't sleep and just cried about the poor man who was dying of AIDS. Now whenever the song comes on the radio he starts to cry.

FAMILY OF JOHN: 8 YEARS

Mother: He does funny things too like sitting on the chair and then he starts to get off and says, 'No John, no John, back on the chair.' He goes through this whole dialogue.

Sister: And when he hit, we used to have to hold his hands on the wall and count to ten. Mum used to get to about eight and then John would try to pull his hands off and Mum would say, 'We're nearly at ten, John.' Now John does it himself. He goes 'One, two, three' then he gets to eight and he starts to pull his hands away and says, 'No John, we're nearly at ten now.' Then he takes his hands off the wall and he says, 'Now John, no more hitting.' Then he'll hit himself and hit himself back, then he'll go on the wall and he'll keep doing that heaps of times until someone disturbs him.

Mother: He gets stuck on things because he can't stop himself. The hitting is not as much of an issue now as it was. The last couple of months he's improved. It still flares up but for a year or so it was a real issue. It was really quite bad but it's really improved.

PARENTS OF RICHARD: 11 YEARS

Mother: At an interview with Tony Attwood (clinical psychologist) he suggested that Richard learn Tai Chi. It took me a while to find lessons, but he has been going once a week now for two months and he loves it. He never forgets and if we do, about 5 minutes before 7.00pm he says, 'Come on Dad, take me to Tai Chi'. It starts about 7.00pm. All the people there really seem to like him. They are all older, up to about 60, I'd say. The teacher says he's doing well.

MOTHER OF KEVIN: 30 YEARS

A couple of years ago, he was undergoing psychological counselling and he was told to paint and draw. Now Kevin has never shown any inclination. He's like me, a stick man is about the limit. But anyway, he had a great, big, old end of newsprint that we've had ever since he was young and he ripped off pieces and actually started painting. Now terribly childlike, very, very basic, a tree is a trunk and a piece of green triangle on the top but he became quite prolific. He just painted and painted and painted, so it's obviously an outlet. But unfortunately he hasn't kept it up. I wouldn't push it because he is now so much better. He's beginning to do a few other things so it's probably not important. But I've heard people say that it is an outlet. I find writing an outlet. I like to speak through my hands so I will write a lot. Particularly if someone upsets me or bothers me I'll write it down. He obviously got it out by slapping paint everywhere. He did slap it everywhere I might add. It went everywhere. In fact, in the end we were walking round on permanent newspapers. But even so, it worked. It was quite good.

FAMILY OF JOHN: 8 YEARS

Mother: We went through a whole number of years trying different dietary approaches to John's condition. For years I kept a record. I went for a while not letting him have peanut butter and for years I didn't let him have dairy products. I kept a record of how many times he hit that day and how many times he wet his pants and, when he was little, how many times he looked at you, trying to determine if there was a difference. Because you try something and people would say, 'Well, is it making an improvement?' and I couldn't actually tell. It was very subjective. So I tried to keep a record of it all, but I've stopped doing it now.

He was about six and I sent away to the States and I got the vitamin B6. I had kept a record and I had been doing it for some time without the vitamin B6. I had three months supply of it. I put him on them for three months so I could compare how many times he hit or wet his pants, all that sort of stuff, and then I did three months without it and three months with it again. After that I came to the conclusion it didn't make any difference. But for some children it does make a difference whereas I think if I hadn't been doing that, I might have been more inclined to say, 'He does seem a lot better or a lot calmer,' because a lot of it is really subjective.

PARENTS OF JENNY: 2 YEARS

Mother: She's got a definite allergy to dairy food: cheese, milk, goat's milk. The only thing she can drink is soya milk. That made quite a difference. I tried everything. She had goat's milk, she had it for three minutes and then she started sneezing and I thought here we go. Two minutes later and up it all came. It's not actually an allergy, she gets a rash and it just comes straight back up. She can cope with a little bit of cheese or a little bit of mashed potato with milk in the potato and a bit of butter, which she absolutely loves. But she is a fussy eater. She won't eat anything that she doesn't want to.

Father: She loves McDonald's. I took a McDonald's bag out of my car and put it in the garage and she saw it a couple of days later. She got it and came running inside with it. She likes chips and things that she can feed herself. One of the joys for us at mealtime is being able to put a table and chair up against the wall and put a plate down with some chicken pieces and some chips and she feeds herself. That's why we have chicken and things like that quite frequently. She doesn't really like fruit. She likes bananas but she doesn't like apples or oranges. She likes muesli bars, sandwiches, that type of thing. She loves her cereal in the morning and toast, she likes toast. And the interesting thing too is that she likes some of the foods that you think a kid wouldn't like, namely bacon, smoked fish, things with garlic in them. I brought home some really strong smoked trout. She loved it, she just hoed into it. She doesn't mind a bit of kebab that has been marinated in garlic and soya sauce, she enjoys it. Sometimes she sits with us when eating, other times we have her at her table and chair.

FAMILY OF JOHN: 8 YEARS

Mother: Poor John, I put him through all sorts of diets. You get really hopeful because you think if it was simply a reaction to certain food that makes him angry then it would be simple: you just wouldn't give it to him. Unfortunately nothing has shown up that clearly.

PARENTS OF JENNY: 2 YEARS

Father: The one time we were really successful with her eating was when we had her cousin around who is two weeks older than her. The two of them don't really get on. She doesn't really have a lot of time for him, typical two-year-olds. He's a boisterous boy and he kept nicking her stuff. Now that she's going to kindergarten, she's become more tolerant of other children. But he was sitting at her little table with the chair and we put Jenny in the chair and the two of them sat there. She sat there all the time that her cousin sat there eating and she ate properly without picking her plate up or throwing her food around or anything. She sat there and ate.

MOTHER OF MICHAEL: 4 YEARS

He's a lot more willing to let me read him a new story than he used to be. You'll find, lying around this house, a page of a book. It's been reduced to that because it's worn out. Even though it's only one page, luckily I know the story. So there's a whole new replenishment of books that's going to come up between now and Christmas. But he definitely has his favourite books and it's still very difficult for me to read him new books. A lot of his books that my father's bought him are unused because it's the same old one over and over again. I actually have to make a deliberate attempt to sit him down, get him sitting while I read him a new story while he goes 'uhuhuh' wanting the other one. But the second time that I'm reading him a new story, he's actually a lot better. By the third time, he's actually asking for it. But the initial attempt to read him a new story is very hard work.

FAMILY OF DAVID: 8 YEARS

Grandmother: The thing was too that we had to teach him everything. Things that we didn't realize, that children pick up by watching. One day we were at the swimming pool. We were in the children's pool and I was walking with David. He didn't want to learn to swim. He just wanted to walk round and round in the pool. Then he fell over. He just stayed there under the water. I had to pull him up. I thought naturally if he went under, he would get up, but he didn't. I had to say to him, 'If you fall over, you have to get straight back up again.' I couldn't believe that it wasn't a natural thing for him to do.

PARENTS OF ALEX: 7 YEARS

Mother: Alex is not allowed to cross the road. And actually that was simple enough to do. It was a friend's suggestion because she was just going straight out onto the road and across and trying to go up to the playground. So we just got a big fat piece of chalk and wrote, 'Stop, No, Stop' on the driveway leading onto the road and she's never crossed the road again.

Father: So she rides her bike just up and down the footpath then she just swivels round on the driveway. She doesn't touch the road. Then she comes back again right over the neighbour's garden!

FAMILY OF DAVID: 8 YEARS

Mother: What David needs now is to get into a group or club where he's going to meet people and learn social skills. They still are not very good. But that is what he needs. Athletics might be good because he could just run; he'd be on his own and he would still have contact with other people. So we may look at that. Gymnastics was not successful at the time but we may try that again.

I notice when we're out, if there are other children, he still doesn't know how to approach them. He still says silly things and doesn't know how to start a conversation. He can't initiate a game. He also misunderstands what some children say to him at school and he takes it as an offence whereas half the time it's just a joke. He is getting better, but he still has problems understanding jokes. Also he was completely literal. He took everything literally and would take things out of all proportion. He is also very straight. He doesn't have the ability to lie which can get him into trouble at times. You couldn't tell him anything, but now you can sit and talk to him. He has an unusual way of looking at things too. Instead of saying 'Turn the light on' he would say, 'Can you turn the dark off'.

PARENTS OF ALEX: 7 YEARS

Mother: Sometimes the children are a bit frightened of Alex because she can be a bit rough sometimes. She thinks that if you hit somebody, they'll start playing. Well, they do, they start to chase you because they want to wallop you back. That's just one of the ways in which she just doesn't get the rules right. She can see cause and effect, 'if you hit, they'll chase, so therefore we must be playing and having a good time'. But she doesn't understand the emotions that go behind it. So sometimes she'll go up and hit but it's an inappropriate way to start to play.

Water is a great leveller. In water Alex is like a mermaid. In actual fact, Alex taken to the beach or to a swimming pool is a really neat way of getting other children to play. Well, not play, but simply share the same environment and have a good time.

FAMILY OF JOHN: 8 YEARS

Mother: He is getting to the stage where he realizes he is different. He can get quite depressed about it. But he doesn't know how to deal with it. And he talks about other children at the Special School too. He wants to know why they can't talk and why some in wheelchairs can't walk and he's concerned about them. So he's aware there are children who differ. There's a boy in his class now who doesn't talk and he asks, 'Why can't he talk?' And I said to him the other day, 'When you were a little boy, you didn't know how to talk properly either.' And he said, 'Why didn't I?' He seems to have an appreciation that there is something going on, why is he different? It's a growing thing but I think he needs that. It's something he has to face.

When he was at the local school, some of the children that he first encountered used to call him 'a handicap' and it's a term that got used at the school. The teacher talked about it but he came home from school and asked, 'Why am I a handicap?' He is certainly wondering about it. The children at the swimming pool were calling him a mental kid which upset me. I have blown my top at the children. It is understandable that they do it but at the same time you get very defensive of him. John laughed at the boys the other day because they were laughing at him and he laughed back. I don't know whether he understood that they were teasing him, whether he just joined in to be part of it. I think embarrassment is not something that's happened to him yet. In some ways I wish it did because then it may help him to not be so embarrassing in public. But that hasn't come to him.

MOTHER OF KEVIN: 30 YEARS

He has a car which he bought. I know people say, 'I suppose you got him that,' but I didn't. Anything the boys have ever had they have literally paid for. We never bought them anything. They had to earn it. And he paid for the car and then he just put his money away. He still does. He'll sit and look at this bank statement and say, 'I've got 100 more dollars' and that's all. He won't use it, unfortunately. I don't think he's tight. I just think he thinks it's there to build up, but he doesn't know what to do with it. Unfortunately he doesn't really know how to enjoy anything like that but, still, we work on that.

PARENTS OF ALEX: 7 YEARS

Mother: There she was, riding her two-wheeler with the trainer wheels, well, one day one of the trainer wheels fell off. We're not a family who have great skills in fixing things and I said to my husband, 'Well, that's the end of riding the bike really. She won't be able to ride the bike.' And within two days she was riding the bike, no trainer wheels. And so it wasn't us saying, 'What can Alex do next?' It was really a series of accidents that challenged us to give her the freedom and she acquired the skills and rose to the occasion.

MOTHER OF MICHAEL: 4 YEARS

He's accomplishing a great deal in the child care centres and with different workers that he's got. Even with the woman who does shared care, who comes here to look after him. He is now going into her house, playing with her cats, watching her television with no dependence on the videos that he's got at home.

She's been able to gradually expand his environment, but it's got to be gradual. I can't spontaneously say, 'Hey, let's go to a movie.' I have to carefully plan everything and so long as I do that, I find that he is a happy chappy.

I've adopted very much a 'go with the flow' approach and I find it creates a calm, happy environment where little things don't matter. I think parents of any child with a disability develop an odd sense of perspective and sense of humour that keeps their nerves firmly rooted in their nerve sockets.

CHAPTER 6

'We respect her right to be different'

It is generally agreed, by families and all those assisting the child, that it is necessary to teach certain skills in order for the child to cope with the demands and accepted 'rules' of society. A child with autism spectrum disorder is, however, different and experiences the world in a unique manner. They therefore have very specific needs, likes and dislikes. In our quest to assist the child to cope with everyday life and learn what we perceive to be the necessary skills, we must not destroy their individuality. Therefore, instead of constantly trying to change the child's behaviour, it is kinder and more beneficial, for all involved, to respect some of those needs and accommodate the 'preferences' as much as possible, whenever it is appropriate. This often involves a lot of trust on the part of the parents and tolerance on the part of the whole family.

MOTHER OF MICHAEL: 4 YEARS

I felt better in myself and we got on much better when I didn't force him into the so-called normal life, without me forcing him to do things he didn't want to do.

I have to make sure that I anticipate everything during the day as far as he is concerned. Where everything is going according to plan, he knows what's happening, he's very happy.

Like last week we went to the school fair. Normally I would've said, 'Come, stay with me. I want to look at the things. I want to buy something,' and force him into the middle of the school fair. But no. We went around the outside of the whole fair and stayed right on the edge of it for an hour while my mother went shopping. That side of life makes it a lot easier because I understand that he doesn't want to go right in the middle. He doesn't want to join in. He can't handle it. That's fine. Whereas before, I would be trying to make him fit in. Trying to get him to do things which just 'freak' him and wondering why I had this nightmare on my hands.

MOTHER OF JOSEPH: 7 YEARS

He has autism and he enjoys things differently than we do, so we have to let him do things differently sometimes. We can't make him normal. I've seen people try and make their autistic children normal and they just lead a miserable existence really. He has to be accepted for who he is. He's a person and he has to have as much right to enjoy the things he enjoys as we have to enjoy the things we enjoy. Just because it's different doesn't mean it's not right. We all have different personalities. We tend to think, because they're autistic they don't have individual personalities. But they do. They might be strong-minded and it's not being autistic, it's just because they have a strong-minded personality. You tend to forget that and people put everything down to autism.

PARENTS OF RICHARD: 11 YEARS

Mother: The biggest problem when we first found out about Richard's disability was ourselves. We adapted over the years and have just accepted him as a person at whatever stage he was at, regardless of whether he was half there or whatever the stage. We don't compare him with others. We compare him with himself, how he was before, mentally we note that he's improved.

PARENTS OF ALEX: 7 YEARS

Mother: She never ceases to amaze me in what she can do. We're immensely proud of her and we know that given the expectations of what we expect from her, that she is placed under enormous stress on a day-to-day basis. Particularly with the issue of being sent to school. We're surprised that we don't have more challenging behaviour because of those stress levels.

The fact that she takes on board an enormous number of incomprehensible social rules that seem to be there for no other reason other than someone has arbitrarily made them. We're enormously proud of her.

FAMILY OF JOHN: 8 YEARS

Mother: After school he's had it. He's obviously passed his best and he doesn't communicate very well at all and he'll spend an hour or two sometimes on the trampoline. The trampoline is brilliant then, which is really good because I can see him out the window too. He goes really high and claps. He does little runs with his feet while he's up there. He loves it.

Sister: He quite likes the trampoline. Sometimes I've knocked on the window and said, 'It's teatime' and he just ignores me, even if he can hear me really clearly. I have to actually go outside and tell him, 'It's teatime, John' and he won't come. Then you say 'Hey, John, do you want to come and have sausages for dinner?' and John will say, 'Yes.'

Mother: You have to be specific.

Father: You also have to use a magnet strong enough to draw him out of the little world of his own. Sausages is good enough.

MOTHER OF MICHAEL: 4 YEARS

My family accepted the diagnosis very, very well. My family were hanging out for a diagnosis probably more than I was, or at least as much as, anyway. When you're a parent you don't spend your life wondering what's wrong with your child. You take it as it comes, you take what you get, you take what you're given. But I was really wanting to know as far as I could, what his problem was, if there was a problem or if there wasn't a problem. I was getting so much conflicting information and ideas and advice because the diagnosis hadn't been made and so it became a problem as to how to develop him. But everybody reacted well as far as I know, to know that there was something identifiable. Yes, I think they reacted quite positively and quite supportively and I felt better being able to say, 'Look, this is his problem. This is why sometimes we have to make allowances for him and we have to make accommodations and we have to accept certain behaviours from him that we wouldn't accept in other children.' That I was able to say, 'This is what it is and this is why. It's not that I've brought him up badly'.

FAMILY OF JOHN: 8 YEARS

Mother: You have to plan. I have a couple of college girls doing their 'Duke of Edinburgh Award', who come two afternoons a week after school. They'll come to take John for a walk, to take him for an outing if he doesn't fit in with the things I need to do. When you go out he takes over everything. So I have someone else to take him out specifically just to keep him happy. If you try and fit him into your routine, then you get explosions. It does depend on his mood. You have to plan things like that to keep the peace to avoid a situation where he's likely to blow his top.

A lot of living with John is learning the techniques that will keep him happy. Like if he says, 'Why can't I go to K...?' A particular beach he likes. If you say to him, 'John, I can take you to K... in four days,' he's happy. Then the next day, he'll say 'In three days we're going to K...' If it's concrete. Every weekend we go to this particular beach at the moment. But if it's just a 'No, you can't go. I'm busy,' that just makes him wild. But if I say to him, 'John would you like to go to K... in four days?' then he's happy. He can count things down from hundreds.

Sister: He's done it for Christmas. He started counting down for Christmas in September.

PARENTS OF ALEX: 7 YEARS

Mother: She challenged our acceptance of her disability and where we saw her limitations by shifting here, and it was simply because of a change in physical environment. I think it was her problem-solving skills again that opened up huge horizons for her.

Father: Also the environment here made it easy for her to get out because it was flat and also because there were more footpaths for her to ride on. So it was more secure than it was at our other house. And we could see her from a distance. We can see 100 yards down the street that way and 50 yards back to the corner that way. And so she did challenge it.

FAMILY OF JOHN: 8 YEARS

Father: He's started running away again lately. When he was little he used to run away, but now he bikes away. That's our biggest issue at the moment. Fortunately at the moment, he bikes back too. He does the round trip. He's very much into direction, where things are and which way and he knows the way. If we don't let him go, he'll just get really angry and go anyway. He's got to an age where you can't keep him shut in unless you want to live in a fort or you want to have him screaming and getting wild all the time. So he has to learn the safety rules. It's true with any child. You have to determine how much lead you give them and how wide their boundaries can be.

He has learnt to wear his helmet. He can go right round the block which he's done several times. We may give him more freedom than other people would. I suppose that's true again with normal children, but there have been the odd occasions where someone has called by and said, 'Do you know John is around the other side of the town?' It's quite a long way round. So that's something we have to keep an eye on.

PARENTS OF ALEX: 7 YEARS

Mother: When we first shifted here, we were so paranoid about her escaping, that we spent a lot of money getting locks on all the doors. After doing that, we found Alex out on the street the next morning, half past six, playing. She had selected the right key to unlock the door to the garage and pushed the button to activate the garage door to get out. So we got an electrician in to cut the wire and the next morning she was out in the street at half past six. She had unlocked the garage door and then selected the correct car key to unlock the car and then got the remote control inside the car. So the third morning we hid the remote control in the house and she simply used fairly logical problem solving and looked in all the places you might hide a remote control, until she found it and she was out in the street at 6.30 in the morning. The fourth morning we decided there wasn't any more we could do, we had to let her go. She had a magic Christmas holiday.

FAMILY OF JOHN: 8 YEARS

Father: I don't know whether people think I'm being irresponsible or cavalier. But then it gets to a point where you have to start trusting him. All these places are places that I've taken him to over and over and he knows the way and he knows the procedures of what goes on there.

It's always a risk because with John, he's unpredictable. I mean he likes the set route. He likes to go to the same places over again, things like that, but at the same time it doesn't take much for him to blow his top. But it's always a risk because you don't know what he's going to do when you're not with him.

PARENTS OF ALEX: 7 YEARS

Father: We've learnt not to underestimate her and everything that she's done. Every time we believe we're running into another problem she seems somehow to solve it.

Mother: I have enormous expectations for Alex. I don't dare to dream too far into the future. We don't set goals too far into the distant future and we tend to follow where Alex leads. And it's taken us on some interesting paths.

Regardless of what the books say, she is quite capable of lying and being devious. She saw that her sister had things in her lunchbox that she didn't, so she swapped the biscuits over. Every morning she goes through her lunchbox and checks to see what's in it which is exactly what any self-respecting seven-year-old does.

There's a lot of normal behaviour going on all mixed up with behaviour that's caused by the autism and I still believe that if you have a profound understanding of the autism, it makes home life easier. You can accept the behaviours.

What family would sit at the dinner table and plunge themselves into darkness because being in darkness was a reward for Alex at that time. So if she was sitting at the table, we would turn the lights out. Actually the sensory deprivation of eating when you can't see what you're eating is quite profound. Then when she left the table, the lights would go back on. We were sitting in our backless chairs because all the spindles had been broken. Alex had been through a rather violent stage at the age of three. We've only just had our chairs and dining room table fixed as well.

FAMILY OF JOHN: 8 YEARS

Mother: We have a unicycle. It was very difficult to find, but we have one. He was obsessed with unicycles. After the microphones, it was unicycles. He chooses weird things to be obsessed with. But he went on and on about unicycles. I actually got given a unicycle for my birthday to keep him quiet, because he had had his birthday and had got a microphone stand, which was what he was obsessed with at that time. As soon as he got it, though, he switched. That's the problem. As soon as he's got something, he switches. He switched to unicycles. You don't want to give him something because he's going on like that, yet you know that if we acquired one in our family, our life would be a lot better. I thought, I can't listen to him going on about it till Christmas, because he's had to learn too that you can't just get what you want. You get something at Christmas and your birthday. So I asked my husband to get me a unicycle for my birthday. I can't ride it, but it's meant he's stopped ranting and raving about unicycles. He did ride it for a while.

PARENTS OF ALEX: 7 YEARS

Mother: Alex doesn't like wearing clothes. This year, she will wear clothes but she won't wear knickers. One of the things she does is pull her pants down so they sit just underneath her bottom so that her bottom makes contact with the tactile experience it happens to be sitting upon. And she will do that in the car.

Because she hates her school uniform, she will get changed from her school clothes into her home clothes in the back seat of the car, to her ten-year-old sister's intense embarrassment. Now if I was parenting a normal child, I would simply not allow that to happen and I guess that's one of the ways that we accommodate her differences. I will tolerate that. If she will tolerate her school uniform all day, I will tolerate a little bit of embarrassment while she flashes herself in the back seat to the entire school population walking by, when she gets changed.

One of the other things she does is she hides the clothes and we can't find the blessed things. So we hide them now. I currently have them hidden in the hot water cupboard stashed underneath a tablecloth and that's worked for the last two mornings. We also started to tell a fib and told her that the teacher whom she currently has an obsession with thought that she just looked beautiful in her winter school uniform. It has improved to the point where she will put her uniform on before her dad leaves for work. Prior to that she would lurch her body on the floor and kick and scream and have a fully fledged tantrum.

I really think what's happening is Alex still has an impaired sensory system. There is something about the materials in the winter uniform that irritates her. She really doesn't like the sensation.

MOTHER OF KEVIN: 30 YEARS

Kevin is incredibly untidy. I don't know whether this is something these children are. You wouldn't expect it from somebody who spent all his childhood agitated by anything at all that was out of place, out of line. All the furniture used to be lined up, all the toys, not that he played with them as toys, but he used to empty out the boys' toy box and put these long lines of things right through the house. Heaven help anybody who kicked anything out of place because he'd go berserk. But he lives in the most incredible muddle. They all have a room and Kevin's room looks as though a bomb has exploded in it every morning to make sure that it always looks like that. He has boxes and paper and dockets. Washing, which he does, they have to do their own washing and they do the cooking, they do everything by roster. They are not allowed to leave dirty washing around but Kevin doesn't put it in a pile. I mean you'll find socks under the bed and pants on the door handle and a shirt may be wrapped around the television. I mean it's just unbelievable that he can live in that state and yet it seems to be something that's become part and parcel of his adulthood. As though all the jumble and the problems and the muddle in this mind manifest themselves in one room. Anywhere else, he's OK. When he comes here, he'll get out books and things but he'll put them back again. But in his room, everything is on the floor. Nothing is in anything, and he just lives like that. Fortunately, although they do ask for a standard and they ask them to clear their rooms out, the people tolerate it. They know that that's him. And obviously that has to be his little secure world of shambles. He just doesn't seem to see it. But he's comfortable, so that I suppose is the main thing.

PARENTS OF ALEX: 7 YEARS

Mother: We do have very high expectations of behaviour for Alex. She has to realize that we have rights and thoughts and feelings and she has to respect our needs just as much as we have to work our way around hers. One of the small family adaptations, we walk around her 'potion pot' (a bowl of leaves, flowers and water), even the two-year-old. Occasionally he has a furtive stir when she's at school but the rest of the time, he respects the fact that her potion pot sits on the bathroom floor.

Alex has all her toys on the floor in her bedroom in rows or categories or whatever she happens to be currently working through, buzz groups or circles, whatever the current theme is. Now he doesn't go in there and play with those, or pick them up. He has already taken on board and accommodated the fact that they are Alex's and they are important to her. And we haven't had to enforce that rule. There is an enormous amount that isn't normal and we respect her right to be different.

CHAPTER 7

'You need to have somewhere to offload'

Parents constantly act as advocates for their child, yet they themselves can be left feeling isolated and excluded. When dealing with the needs of their child, parents also want to feel that they are being listened to and assisted. They need to feel supported and not judged and to feel that professionals are also considering their needs as well as those of their child.

In order to cope with the demands of a child with autism spectrum disorder, it is essential that parents feel included and supported by family, professionals and society. They need to be able to go somewhere where they can relax and feel that they are understood and accepted, whether it is a family group or supportive organization.

Mother of Joseph: 7 years

One of the advantages of living down here, the reason we moved, is to be close to my family. They're really understanding about Joseph and really supportive. I mean, he goes and pours red wine over their lounge suite and they say, 'It's all right, dear. You have to expect that when you've got an autistic grandson.' You think, really they'd like to say, 'Would you shift back to the city.' But they'd never say that. They're really good. And it's nice for Joseph. It takes some of the responsibility off us. I mean, we still have the ultimate responsibility, but we can share the load a bit more. If there's a problem, they're racking their brains along with us. Just things like that. I can go to their home and just relax and not be running around thinking where Joseph is and what's he doing? They've got locks on all their doors so he can only be in the lounge or in the kitchen. He likes to hop into beds and he just wrecks room after room basically. He pulls beds to bits and empties make-up bags and bottles of perfume.

When Joseph comes in, Mum whips up the hallway and snips all the locks and so you go there and you can relax. They accept that Joseph is part of the family and that's just part of how they accept responsibility for that too. It's one of those things that comes with being a grandmother or an aunty, so we're very, very lucky.

Family of David: 8 years

Mother: When he was born, instead of the doctor saying, 'It's a girl or it's a boy,' he said, 'Oh, that's a very good looking baby.' That's the first thing he said and I've never forgotten that. I thought, 'That's a strange thing to say.'

PARENTS OF JENNY: 2 YEARS

Father: She was a normal baby. She was a really good kid, if a little too good. We really had no problems with her. Between about 13 and 15 months of age I think we noticed something wrong. And then it was like the door shut, bang. It was like she was dead.

She was never a really cuddly baby. It was her attention span and her hearing that concerned us. We went to the audiology clinic and they found nothing wrong with her ears or hearing.

Mother: Before we found out, when Jenny was going through her hearing tests, Mum actually said, 'I think she's autistic.' She's worked in a community home where there are autistic adults. But I didn't know much about it. 'Autistic tendencies' is what we were told. We were told over the phone. Our paediatrician was supposed to get back to us with blood test results and chromosome tests, but he never did. So I kept ringing and ringing and in the end my husband wrote him a letter.

Father: The paediatrician rang me after he received the letter and said that this is what she'd got. We were not taken into a doctor's room and told, 'This is what we believe the situation is. We believe she's autistic or has autistic tendencies. This is what you could expect.' Yet if Jenny had a brain tumour, we would have been in there the next day. We would have been in that office and told, 'Your daughter has a brain tumour. These are the choices in treatment; what do you think we should do?' Yet where we are at the moment, I can't see the difference between her being autistic or having a brain tumour. There was no communication there at all. Probably because it's not an exact science.

PARENTS OF ELEANOR: 7 YEARS

Mother: It's the parents who need the help, instantly. You are the ones whose lives have been shattered, not your child. It's you two who are the ones who need to be picked up and put back together again, because it's you two who have just been destroyed.

Nothing has changed for the child. Instant marriage guidance counselling is needed for a start, to tell parents that from now on you are going to be under indescribable pressure and grief, which may well drive a wedge between you and eventually destroy your relationship.

The parents have got to stick together for the child. I have heard that 60 per cent of all marriages where there is a disabled child break up. Why do so many marriages disintegrate? Because none of the couples have been told, 'Beware.' They have to be told, 'Look, you're going to grieve at different times and in different ways, so you're going to have to get used to the cycles of grief in each other. You're going to have to learn to read the other person and to back off when they're in a bad way. You have to therefore lift yourself up and give support when you can and receive it when it is given.' If my husband is really having a tough time with Eleanor and finding it hard, I have got to stop finding it hard for those few days and lighten up. Both of us can't be down at the same time and it takes a long time to learn that. So you say, 'Why don't I put Eleanor to bed tonight and you can settle the toddler.' Just simple. It's balance, balance, balance.

PARENTS OF JENNY: 2 YEARS

Mother: I only go and visit people that I know haven't got precious things around the house or can close off a room. We don't visit very often. If we do, it's my parents' place who are used to her. We can't take her anywhere that hasn't got a fence either. We've got a few safe houses where we can basically go in, shut the doors and we know that she's not going to get into anything and if she does and breaks something, it's not really a big problem.

We can't really go round to people we don't know that well, if she'll run riot. They wouldn't invite us back again. That probably is one of the hardest things we've found.

Father: We keep the masking tape people in business, as you can see around the place. All the drawers and cupboards around the house are either closed with masking tape or elastic bands so she can't get into them. We're going to get some door catches. She doesn't even try the ones with the latches because she knows she can't get into them.

Mother: I don't like leaving people with Jenny, because I know what she's like and I don't think that anyone else should have to put up with it. And Jenny withdraws when she is not well supervized. But there are a few people, like my brother, who really adore her. She really likes him as well. He comes around quite a bit. He only works down the road. He comes straight up from work and can stay the night which is great.

PARENTS OF ELEANOR: 7 YEARS

Mother: The parents are the two most important people. Get the parents functioning again and give them regular counselling. Someone to go to and talk to, to say, 'We are finding this impossible. Is this normal? Do other people feel this?' A trained person who is a parent, who comes with a professional so that they can balance one another, so that there is the professional point of view, 'What we're going to do for the child; what we're going to do for you; what help there is available.' But also to get the personal point of view from the parent saying, 'Look, we've been there, we're still married. We go out for dinner in the evenings. It's OK. Yes, there is life after autism.'

Parents know the sort of questions that parents will be thinking. What they need to hear immediately are the nice things; that their children are pretty; that the children have normal bedrooms; because you only think of the bad things. 'Will I ever be able to leave the house again?' 'Will my life ever be reasonably normal again?'

MOTHER OF KEVIN: 30 YEARS

I always remember a psychologist, one of the many, saying to me when Kevin was quite young he realized that these children are actually the end result of the parents who are cold and I thought, 'Gosh, how ironic.' I wonder if she'd ever thought of coming and living in our household. We used to be a very raucous household, a very physical household. My husband and I were always very physical people, which is probably why I found it very hard. Everyone finds it hard to adjust after someone dies but that's what I miss more than anything, the touching and the loving. But I found that I had become the autistic person, because I had to shut myself away so that I could cope with Kevin once I was by myself.

PARENTS OF JENNY: 2 YEARS

Father: I think we need a central diagnostic centre where they put the children through an assessment. It would be nice to be able to have Jenny go somewhere for a day and be tested or whatever she needs and someone would say, 'On a scale of 1 to 10 in autism terms, she is a 2 or 3 or 10. This means that this will happen and the possible outcomes are: if she regresses she will end up here; if she improves she'll end up here; and if she stays the same this is what you can expect.'

At this stage, you just cope from day to day. You don't have a lot of opportunity to plan ahead. We're thinking, 'Well, is Jenny going to be with us when she is 18? Is she going to be in a position to live her own life in a normal way? Are we going to have to look at an IHC home? What are the options? Do we have more children?' We can't plan too far ahead. It's very difficult and I know those questions are almost impossible to answer. On the other hand, that would be the perfect scenario.

MOTHER OF JOSEPH: 7 YEARS

It can just get too much. You just get that you can't think your way out of it any more and you get bogged down by it. I used to feel the 'I'm a prisoner in my own home' syndrome. You feel like you are because to go anywhere is very difficult so you stay home. As a mother it tends to be you're the one that stays at home and that's your life, you and Joseph.

I think I'd be quite bitter and angry if I didn't have that support. You need to have somewhere to offload, with some-one to talk to, and I think if I didn't, I'd stew it up inside. It would be easy to resent everyone for what they've got and you haven't. But I just go over there (parents' home), tell them all about it and have a bawl or whatever. I don't now so much. Shows that I've got the right amount of support. But before, when Joseph wasn't very well and I didn't have much support, I was going up there often because it just got too much for me.

But he's pretty good now and we've got a lot more sup-port. I rang the IHC bawling my eyes out after Easter. It was a long Easter and he was at his worst. He hadn't had his seizure, but he was building up to it and fortunately the lady at the IHC had a lot to do with autistic children so she knew straight away that I meant it.

PARENTS OF ELEANOR: 7 YEARS

Mother: I felt that everyone was there for the child but no-one was there for the parents. Initially that was partly my fault. I didn't want to know about the Autistic Association. I didn't want to know that I was a member of a club that I didn't want to be a member of and I had been made a life member of the Autistic Association. I just didn't want to know about it.

Father: This was something where we disagreed. I wanted to find out more about it and find out what the long-term future was, but my wife didn't want to know.

Mother: I still don't always want to know. To my way of thinking, there's no point in looking at older people because each autistic person is such an individual. Although there are certain characteristics they all share, each one will develop into a completely original adult. I found it much more helpful to watch and try to accept my own child for what she is right now and leave the future to unfold as it will.

PARENTS OF JENNY: 2 YEARS

Father: I don't lose sleep over why it happened. It's just one of those things. It's wonderful to read the books and read the stories of people who have put the time and years and effort into the children. The children show results. Sometimes I question, 'Are we doing enough?' but at the end of the day, all you're doing is just coping and surviving. You've got no energy left to do anything. You've got no energy at all at the weekend. Sometimes you're so frazzled and you're so frustrated and on edge and stressed out, that what you want to do is put Jenny in the room, shut the door and forget about her for three hours so you can sit and relax. But you can't do that.

I'd love to have the endless energy to be able to spend all my waking hours giving Jenny therapy, but it just unfortunately doesn't work like that.

PARENTS OF ELEANOR: 7 YEARS

Mother: The professionals we've had dealings with are a mixed and varied bunch. When they're good, they're very, very good and when they're bad, they're absolutely ghastly. They have more impact on your life than they know actually. Professionals have no notion generally at all what an appalling sentence has been passed on parents when their child is diagnosed with autism. They have no notion what they're doing when they utter the words, 'I think your child is autistic.' They are destroying your world. It's like a bomb has dropped and what they're leaving behind is devastation of a kind that parents cannot be prepared for and have never experienced before. You can't just diagnose a child, then say to the parents, 'Now just go home and read books about it.' You can't do that to parents. It shouldn't be allowed. You ask any parent of a child who has been diagnosed with autism and they can usually give you, word for word, exactly what was said to them, what the day was like, what the child was wearing and how they felt, years and years later. You can't remember a lot after those words have been said. For instance, you can't remember how you got home or remember what you said to each other.

MOTHER OF PETER: 17 YEARS

Peter was at risk because of his early convulsions, so we used to go to a paediatrician. He was very negative. When Peter was about two, he said, 'He'll never be physically right all his life.' He obviously had no idea what was wrong with him, no idea what he was like mentally and he threw that one at me. I just got upset. Instead of saying, 'What on earth are you talking about?', I just couldn't. I got upset and I remember crying all the way home. The doctors and psychologists didn't have any idea and they wouldn't admit it. Still they don't have any time for me or Peter. They really just didn't care. No-one did really. No-one cared. Not even my family, no-one helped. The trouble is the more you cope, the more people think you don't need help.

Once when he had a streaming ear infection for two weeks, I remember going to the doctors because he wouldn't take medication. I went to one doctor and he gave me some antibiotics and Peter wouldn't take them. I tried another doctor and another doctor and by about the third doctor I just cracked up. I wish I'd done that more often. I just said, 'None of you doctors care a damn. You just don't care. You're the third one in this practice I've been to and you just keep giving me these goddamned different antibiotics and he won't take them.' I burst into tears and I got instant attention. I had that doctor for years. He was great after that. He kept ringing me up and asking how it was going.

MOTHER OF KEVIN: 30 YEARS

I had a placid, everlastingly sleeping baby who suddenly, at about seven or eight months, started to scream and that was it. He appeared to be normal at birth. He reached the stage where he was rolling over and lying on his tummy and laughing at things and then he became remote. We realized there was something wrong. I spoke with the doctor (he's known me ever since I was a young person) and he said, 'Well, I'd follow up. I do think that it's not something that you should just leave.' So I did, but not with any great success. Professional people would push me off and say, 'Well, I don't think there's anything basically wrong. He's a baby that's perhaps a bit temperamental. Are you feeding him right?'

One psychologist specifically said to me, 'Do you realize you have a shrill voice?' to which I pointed out that if she'd had to live in a house with a child that had screamed non-stop for a couple of months, she would have had a shrill voice too. But she didn't appreciate that. Kevin was meanwhile opening and shutting her file drawer to the point where I think she thought it was going to go through the wall. I did say, 'Well, this constant behavioural activity is the sort of thing he does. It's not just banging the door like babies do.' I said, 'Twenty-four hours round the clock he will be banging a door.' However, I was very gently fobbed off from that and I went through the different channels. I really got nowhere.

PARENTS OF JENNY: 2 YEARS

Father: The most difficult thing about having a child with autism is there's never a quiet time. Until she's asleep at night there's never an opportunity to put her in her room for an hour or, 'Oh, she's sitting on the couch reading a book,' or 'She's playing with something.' That for me is the big thing. You can't just have a ten-minute sit down with a magazine and a cup of coffee because she will try to rip the magazine off you or she's wanting to be picked up, only to want to be put down again. Or she will be at the other end of the house and you won't hear anything. That's suspicious because normally she's making too much noise destroying something.

Mother: The worst thing is not being able to have a breather. It's hard during the day but I go out for a walk or something which I find helps. Jenny often goes to sleep during our walk and going out in the car is great because that's about one of the only places she sleeps aside from her bed. But you can't lift her out, that'll wake her up. So I leave her in the car in the garage and leave the door open.

MOTHER OF KEVIN: 30 YEARS

When Kevin was little, he didn't want to be in the living world with other people. He was perfectly happy if he could be shut in his room or away somewhere in the garden where he didn't have to be disturbed.

A lot of things, I noticed, used to frighten him. The worst part in the bigger supermarkets was the fact that they had a very high ceiling. A lot of things were hanging around and anything that flapped or waved was obviously frightening. Of course I was asked by a professional whether I had frightened him with something at some stage, 'Had there ever been anything hanging in the window or making a noise in the house?' I said 'No, but…' This is what I mean, 'GUILT' in big capital letters. I used to come out of any session I ever had feeling that I had brought this upon myself. But it did ease off. As the time went by and a few more children popped out of the woodwork in the city where we lived, we started to realize that this wasn't just something that the parents were creating. It was a phenomenon that had been around for many years.

PARENTS OF JENNY: 2 YEARS

Father: The girls at work were talking about Jenny yesterday and they were saying, 'Oh, she's the busiest little thing you've ever seen. She doesn't stop.' And it's true. When she's asleep, she's asleep. As soon as her eyes are open she's, bang, up in the bed and off she goes. She doesn't have any dozing period. She only has one speed and that's full on. She's always busy doing something. When she's tired, had a long day, now and again she will lie on the floor for a moment, but she won't stop twitching her leg or moving her head around or whatever. Until she is asleep, she never actually stays in one spot for any length of time.

MOTHER OF KEVIN: 30 YEARS

Kevin had no speech. He would vocalize but it was mostly screaming. He didn't cry as such, he screamed but didn't shed tears, which is apparently quite a common thing but I didn't realize that at the time. I took him to a speech therapist and said, 'Look, I would like some assistance.' The woman sort of looked at me and said, 'Yes dear, you come back when he's got a few words and we'll build on it.' I said, 'But he might never have a few words. We've had no progress up till now,' and she said, 'Well, I don't think I've got a lot to build on at this stage. Do you speak to him?' I said, 'Constantly, and I read to him constantly. I may be sitting in a closed room with the door shut, he's flying round, throwing things, banging his head on the wall and doing something completely obnoxious but I keep reading and sooner or later I'm going to get through to that child.'

Eventually I did find a speech therapist, who said, 'Yes, there's no reason why we shouldn't get some speech,' and she worked on him and I continued to work on him. Over a long period of time, Kevin started to form words; echolalia at first, then with meaning. I don't want to sound as though I was the martyr and I did it all by myself, but I didn't get a lot of assistance from outside, I'm afraid. Not in those days anyway.

PARENTS OF ELEANOR: 7 YEARS

Mother: It's the parents who are diagnosed, not the child. When the child is diagnosed with autism, nothing changes for the child. They just go on their merry way being what they were in the first place. It's the parents who are diagnosed. You are now the parents of an autistic child. It's your diagnosis, not the child's. There must be a more sane, kind way to break this life sentence to the parents.

There must be a gentler way than to just have a complete stranger pass this life sentence of horror upon you. What should happen if there is a suspicion of a diagnosis of autism is that someone should come around to the house and perhaps play with the child and gradually indicate some of the behaviours that are unusual and perhaps offer some constructive advice and gradually move into the diagnosis. That way surely would leave the parents less shattered, would give parents something to hang on to, because you're drowning, you're dying. If you have a nice, sane, pleasant person saying to you, 'What we're going to start doing is to work a little on …', 'We'll have a little bit of time once a week if that suits you. I'll come around and look, she's doing some lovely things here and what we're going to work on is…' If it was introduced like that, it would have to be kinder. There must be a better way than plunging the parents into hell and having to spend the next two years or more trying to get them out of that hell.

MOTHER OF JOSEPH: 7 YEARS

We were lucky. We had quite a smooth diagnosis. I just went to the right place at the right time pretty much, so I didn't really have a problem with that. They didn't say he was autistic. They told me he was 'developmentally delayed' and they waited till I said he was autistic and then after that they said he was autistic. I think it's a bit of a heavy duty label to put on a two and a half year old, so they said 'developmentally delayed' until he's a bit older probably, which is sensible, I suppose, but it's also a little bit hard because it gave you false hope. Well, they can't say what the outcome is, so they don't. At first you are relieved to know what the problem is and that it's not your fault. We felt that if we got a lot of help for Joseph and worked really hard at it, we'd get on top of the problems Joseph had. But then it makes you go off into a little dreamworld about 'this is going to happen', and then all of a sudden you read a few books and you think, 'Oh my God' and you bawl your eyes out.

PARENTS OF ELEANOR: 7 YEARS

Father: We were given a book to read by a parent of an autistic child. She has a lot to say about autism. I can't criticize that; after all she is the parent of an autistic person. But at the same time, it might have paid to be left for a couple of weeks or a month or two after the diagnosis before you wanted to delve in. You should have someone talking to you, not to read about it. I took the book to work and I spent the next hour on the phone to my wife. I was just reading all these points of incredible depression. It was just so terrifying.

It was written about a child who sits in the corner all the time and spins wheels. My child doesn't spin wheels. Her child spent hours stacking and unstacking, my child didn't spend hours stacking and unstacking.

MOTHER OF JOSEPH: 7 YEARS

The professional people that diagnosed Joseph knew their stuff; no-one misled me. However, the professional people who aren't in the field of autism, like the school and the GP and the sort of professionals that you have to deal with in an ongoing way, just don't know anything about autism.

But because they're professionals they feel they have to put on this act, so it's actually worse. I wish they would just say, 'Look, I'm sorry, could you get me some material to read on this?' But a lot of them assume that because they're the professional and have maybe seen one autistic child, Joseph must be like that. It's kind of a power thing where they are the experts, and they don't like to admit that they aren't when it comes to Joseph.

PARENTS OF ELEANOR: 7 YEARS

Mother: There is a need for some form of documentation to give to parents. Something like the Autistic Association pamphlet. That's a reasonably soft introduction. We know now when we read it, we read an awful lot more into the statements that are made in there. But you give that to a person in the street, most of them would look at it and say, 'So what? That doesn't look too bad.' It's not terrifying. There is a need for some literature which may give you a gentle introduction, to give you some sort of inkling as to the sort of effect it can have on your life.

MOTHER OF JOSEPH: 7 YEARS

Joseph goes away every second weekend to his shared care family and stays a Thursday night every week. It sounds a lot but we really need it and we're lucky because they're really good with him. They love him and he's just part of their family too. They've got three older boys, 14, 12 and 10, and they're just great with him. I don't feel bad at all because it's actually Joseph that's winning, because he's got two lots of positive, recharged people rather than just being with us, and us getting worn out and raising our voices to him. That's sort of how we survive now.

MOTHER OF PETER: 17 YEARS

I've always had my own life as well. I've always played sport to really switch off and I really got into bridge too when he was quite young. I always played once a week. I had odd jobs and a good social life so that's probably what kept me going.

PARENTS OF ELEANOR: 7 YEARS

Mother: I found metaphors very helpful when people would ask, 'What's it like? How does it feel?' People who haven't had a lot of grief, or haven't had a handicapped child, just don't understand how it can affect your life. If the child was crippled, they could see the wheelchair, the ramps, but with an 'Eleanor' you can't see, so it's so very hard for an outsider to see the impact on your life.

It's as if you've been put on a tremendously fast racing river and you've been in a very comfortable ocean liner, so you haven't really noticed the river much. Then suddenly the ocean liner crashes and you're left with a piece of wood to float on down this awful river. Then bit by tiny bit, you get other pieces of wood and you make a tiny raft for yourself. And that's a bit more comfortable and better than what you had before. Every once in a while bits fall off the raft and you have to start again but it's never quite the plank of wood you started with; it never gets that bad again. That's how I picture it and it gives me some comfort to realize the progress we have made.

MOTHER OF JOSEPH: 7 YEARS

The most important thing to survival would be support. The kind of support I'm getting now where he's living a family life like kids his age do. That's very important. Because I have seen this year what a disaster not having the support could lead to. It can affect your whole family and just make it disintegrate into nothing.

I miss being in the city where there are other families and I do miss just having someone you can say something really terrible to and they don't look mortified. You can actually laugh about something really horrific. You really care about their kids and they really care about your kid because they understand the battle that you have. So I do miss that.

PARENTS OF JENNY: 2 YEARS

Father: There's no sort of 'you're suddenly an expert'. It doesn't work like that. Half of my role in it is keeping my wife as happy and problem-free, stress-free as possible, otherwise it's a huge challenge on the relationship.

Mother: It is nice having the Autistic Association. I enjoy going to coffee mornings, talking to the other parents and finding out what they do. Some of the things their kids do are quite funny and you just laugh. I've had a few ladies ring up and say that they're there to talk to. They've got older children. So that's great.

It's nice to go to a meeting and look at somebody who sees life in your perspective. You look into their eyes and see that they are actually agreeing with you, 'I know what you're feeling. I know what is going on.' It's also quite positive from our point of view that Jenny, at this stage, is not as severe as some of the other autistic children. That sounds terrible, but you look at some of the other children and they are really seriously autistic and you think, 'Well, we're not that bad after all.' Sitting there, swapping stories is just nice; people know exactly where you're coming from.

CHAPTER 8

'She is so funny and so mischievous'

Despite the common misconception, many of the children with autism spectrum disorder do have, or do develop, a wonderful sense of humour and enjoy the company of other people. Many of the children have loving, often mischievous natures and want to participate in the fun. Families also share experiences of the laughter gained from some unusual situations they have found themselves in, as well as the love shown to them and their child in the various situations throughout their lives.

PARENTS OF ELEANOR: 7 YEARS

Mother: We're now getting some 'warm fuzzies' with Eleanor really. She is very cuddly at the moment, very affectionate. She loves having her back rubbed. If she hears us laughing in the bedroom with the other two children, she always comes in and joins in. She loves staying in the same room with her sister when we're on holiday.

I love this photograph of the girls on the trampoline. Eleanor's smiling. She's looking at the camera and the two girls even look alike. It's just lovely when she's playing with the others and when you look outside and she's having a good time in the hammock with her sister. She's having a wonderful time, whooping with joy and nobody sounds quite as happy as Eleanor does when she's expressing herself. It's as satisfying as hearing a cat purring.

MOTHER OF JOSEPH: 7 YEARS

When Joseph was first diagnosed as autistic, I was just an object and everyone was just an object. He'd live in the corner of the backyard all the time if he could, or in his bedroom, and he'd never look at anyone. But now he knows who we all are. He has a relationship with us and he knows his grandparents and he loves them; you can tell. He'll run up and grin at them and he'll sit on their knee and he'll cuddle them. That's really lovely that we've got that. He likes us and we know he does because he shows us and that's good. You need that back for all you give. He'll look at them and grin at them when they say, 'Hi Joseph.' It gives people warm fuzzies. So that's one of Joseph's strong skills. Joseph is very sociable for an autistic person. He enjoys people. The barbecue last night was great. He loves all the people, the food, it was busy and just the whole atmosphere. He really gets into it. Christmas and birthdays, he just runs around, grinning and sits on everyone's knee which is probably what he'll do when he's 25 and it won't be quite appropriate, but at the moment it's nice.

PARENTS OF JENNY: 2 YEARS

Father: At the time we first found out about her being autistic, she hated being touched. She would squirm and push you away. Now she wants the attention. We would really, really try to make her give us a cuddle. She would try crawling away and you had to hold her really tightly so she couldn't get away. She finally gave up trying. And now she seeks a lot of attention and loves cuddles.

Jenny is quite good associating with people. In fact she is really starting to show off.

PARENTS OF ALEX: 7 YEARS

Father: The children play and horse around together with me. All three of them are now involved and jump on my back. When Alex was diagnosed nearly six years ago, when we did that she would just ignore us, she wouldn't participate. We'd play horsy rides and Alex would just walk out of the room. This was when she was about two or three. It's only since she went to kindergarten and school and has seen how other kids operate, and she so wants to be like them, that she will participate now.

FAMILY OF JOHN: 8 YEARS

Father: He does interrelate quite a lot with the other children, more and more with games and with great hilarity too. It's quite good how he'll do that now.

He's learnt a lot from playing with his little sister too. She plays a lot with him, providing he's in that frame of mind.

MOTHER OF JOSEPH: 7 YEARS

Joseph loves his school mates. He runs into class and loves seeing them all and they're wonderful with him. That's something with mainstreaming. There's just as much advantage for the other kids. They are so understanding and so aware of Joseph. They're more aware than adults are of what Joseph needs and doesn't need, and what he wants now; when to be close to him, and when to move away. They run around and find him sticks to twiddle when he's upset and they'll turn music on and sing him a song when he's upset. They just don't get sick of him or are negative about the chaos he can create. They're wonderful.

MOTHER OF MICHAEL: 4 YEARS

He sleeps like a log. He is really good about going off to bed when it's time. If he's a little bit awake, we'll have stories at bedtime and that's fine, otherwise he's happy for me to put the light out and go off, generally. If he's quite awake, at a suggestion from his education support worker, I've been playing Tchaikovsky on the tape recorder. I've got an old tape from my mother of Swan Lake on one side and Sleeping

Beauty on the other and halfway through this he's snoring. It's hilarious really to see this enormous 'hefalump' snoring away to Swan Lake.

PARENTS OF ALEX: 7 YEARS

Mother: A lot of what Alex sees on television comes through. She appeared in the room the other day and she had on a pair of shorts, a red sunhat, and two pairs of trousers slung over each shoulder that were supposed to represent braces. Apparently according to her sister, it's some character on Saturday morning TV. And the other thing that she is acting out quite frequently at the moment is the disposable nappy advertisement where you put two balloons in a disposable nappy and they prick them to see how absorbent they are. Well, she goes to get one of her little brother's nappies and then she fills up a bathing cap which of course isn't quite like a balloon and is prone to excessive leaking and lays it on the top of the nappy. One presumes she's testing out the absorbability of this disposable nappy. She's very clever. She's realized that it's not incredibly absorbent, particularly when one fills a bathing cap with water, so she'll lay a towel down underneath it. She just picks up the whole sodden mess when she's finished experimenting. What's going through her mind when she does that I don't know. But it's hilarious. Life's fascinating at the moment.

PARENTS OF ELEANOR: 7 YEARS

Father: We put the 'electric fence' up to stop Eleanor climbing the fences and wandering off and to stop her climbing on the fence and then up on the tiled roof of the house. So the pergola was interlaced with electric fence and rose climbers. That's a project that didn't last very long. It didn't work. Eleanor found her way around it. She discovered that if she pulled her sleeves down and clenched her fist, she could climb over it. It was a real exercise watching her climb over it using her elbows and knees. It took her 20 minutes but she got there.

Mother: When Eleanor's sister was first a little 'Brownie', they were talking about electricity and the safety of electricity in the house. The little Brownies were all asked by Brown Owl if they could think of any things that weren't safe in the house that were electric. And all the other children talked about kettles, heaters, power points and my daughter puts up her hand and in a nice brisk voice says, 'Well, you don't want to touch an electric fence.'

'You've got an electric fence?'

'Yes,' she replies, 'it goes all around the garden and you don't want to touch that. That's not safe.' A lovely suburban Brownie pack Brown Owl thinking, 'What do they have an electric fence for?'

I'm afraid the poor little girl doesn't realize just how different her life is. 'Doesn't everyone have an electric fence?'

MOTHER OF KEVIN: 30 YEARS

There was an episode at the school swimming sports (when Kevin was young). They allowed Kevin to go swimming, because all the children went in for everything. Of course he wasn't very co-operative but they got him into the water and he floundered his way to the end of the pool. Two women were sitting by me and one of the women said, 'That's the little boy who creates a few problems,' and my ears sort of went 'tweak'. I was so used to it and I thought, 'What's going to come now?' And she said to the other lady sitting alongside her, 'Well, of course the teacher said something about him being artistic, but artistic my eye, I'm sure my child draws just as well as he does.' I laughed and thought, 'Well, they didn't get that quite right.' I didn't bother to join in the conversation but obviously someone must have said that he was autistic. He never was any good at drawing anyway.

Parents of Jenny: 2 years

Mother: Last night my brother was around here and she really loves him. She was running around, she wouldn't go to sleep. She was banging on the door to get out of her room and when she came out, she was running around showing off, until she went to sleep. When we have visitors around she won't go to sleep, which says to me that she's enough into our world to think, 'Hey, hang on a second, I want to hang around and be part of it.'

Father: She can still at times be withdrawn and quiet. She hasn't withdrawn for quite a while though. But she is certainly much more physical. She will actually give you a kiss.

PARENTS OF ELEANOR: 7 YEARS

Father: One night I heard a thumping noise and I just thought the children were jumping around upstairs. It was in the middle of winter and it was pitch black and there was a knock on the front door. Some fellow I have never seen before said to me, 'Excuse me, your little girl is up on the roof.' My reaction at the time was, 'Oh no, not again.' I realized afterwards that she didn't have any clothes on and here she was singing and doing her little dance along the ridge of the roof.

When we look back over many of these incidences they are a source of great humour.

MOTHER OF MICHAEL: 4 YEARS

He used to just run and hide in my bed under the covers when anyone used to visit. Now he's going to the door and saying 'Hi' and he's greeting everyone with a smile which is marvellous. He's already miles more sociable than he used to be.

I really want to move on that, and then I think more socialization with other children is going to come, because he loves other children. He doesn't always know how to play appropriately with them, but luckily he's not aggressive and they're not scared of him. I can truly say, Michael most of the time is a delight and he is loved totally by all of us. I have learnt so much from him that I'm very glad he picked me to be his Mum.

MOTHER OF PETER: 17 YEARS

You couldn't take him to the movies, which was hard on my other son but I did have a friend who had two sons, so in the holidays she'd take them to a movie. I couldn't take Peter in to a movie theatre. Then he must have been about 11 or 12 and I finally decided I'd try him out. So I went to the manager of the theatre and I explained the situation, 'Could we just sit in the back row. He may only last there five minutes but if he lasts any longer, I'll come and pay you.' He said, 'Sure, that's fine,' and he sat through the whole movie and loved it. The movie was 'Dick Tracy'. And my mother was there. He just absolutely loved it. In the movies he put his arm around me and leaned over and looked right into my eyes. This amazing eye contact, looked right in and smiled at me, looking at me as if to say, 'This is fantastic, this is neat.' He kept doing it, putting his arm round me in the movies and I just sat there. I think I watched him the whole movie. I didn't want to watch Dick Tracy. I just sat there absolutely fascinated and his eyes were just glued to the screen and he was laughing and he'd laugh before everyone else did. It was amazing. He'd get it before anyone else did when it was funny. It was just the most incredible experience. Driving home in the car, because my mother is kind of scared of Peter, she doesn't understand him, she was sitting in the back seat. I was just watching her in the rear vision mirror and he leaned over and he put his arm round my mother and looked her in the eye too and smiled at her. Well, she was just about bawling, she couldn't believe it. I was just about crying driving the car. It was amazing and she said,

'He's never done that, he's never ever touched me.' It was incredible.

PARENTS OF ELEANOR: 7 YEARS

Father: Actually when Eleanor is switched on, she is the most rewarding of the three children to be with because she is so funny and so mischievous. Sometimes she doesn't want to go to bed because she just wants to play games. She'll climb into bed and get underneath the blankets and she'll be giggling and giggling and she won't let you out of the room. She'll grab you and pull you back into the room and she's got a strong grip. She's having a lovely game and she doesn't want it to stop. You really don't want to put her to bed. You want it to continue as long as possible. Now that's not autism. That's Eleanor's personality.

Mother: It's also Eleanor's nature. When she's in a good mood there's no-one more fun to be with. It's like having the beacon of a lighthouse on you; one minute it's there and then it's gone again; but every once in a while it stops on you and it's mesmerizing. She's just wonderful.

PARENTS OF ALEX: 7 YEARS

Mother: Alex's art work in the past started with very fat people drawn with chalk because she had poor grasp and poor 'fine motor' skills. Her art work has really developed on concrete with chalk. We're now getting to the stage where she can draw certain things very accurately. At the moment, it's mushrooms. She's drawn a lot of mushrooms. We have an obsession about mushrooms. She'll draw the same pictures over and over and over.

Over the past two years her pictures of people have become more sophisticated. They now have smiley faces whereas when she first started to draw them, they had this deep, grim slash across the face that just made them look terrifying. I just wondered if that's how she perceived the world. Now everyone's smiling. It's nice.

CHAPTER 9

'He's gone way beyond functioning in society – he's now excelling'

It is impossible to foretell the future. You cannot predict how a child will progress through life. It is just as impossible to predict how a child diagnosed with autism spectrum disorder will develop. There is no typical autistic child, as the children in these interviews prove. They have all developed in unique ways.

So for those of you who wondered at the end of the previous chapter: How are the families now? What happened to the children? Where are they now? What are they doing? What sort of people did they grow up to be? Here are some answers to those questions.

JOHN: 22 YEARS

I'm 22 years old and I'm working for a concrete company on Tuesdays and Fridays. They make concrete slabs and moulding bays and my job has been to drive the pneumatic trolley that goes around and collects all the little bits and prevents the holes being punched into tyres. Thousands of dollars have been saved from tyre punching. I'm working at the local vintage railways on Wednesdays and Saturdays. I work at another vintage railway company doing steam engine restoration in the city. The rail stuff's all voluntary.

One thing that got me a little bit embarrassed was when all the guys knew that I worked at the other vintage railway; they'd seen my article in the local newspaper, and one of them said, 'You're a traitor, working for the opposition.' But we get things like that said to us all through our lives. You've just got to learn to take them with a pinch of salt and not take it too seriously.

I've always been a rail enthusiast. I've been fascinated with trains. I like travelling on them, I like them. Just something I've had enthusiasm with. To relax I drink a beer, I listen to music or play my Xbox or watch a movie. I watch train DVDs. I read my Bible and read books. I don't seem to do a lot of reading. I do like driving places.

I used to love the unicycle and I used to play a lot of music but now I get more into trains as a hobby than music. But I still like listening to music. I still like a variety of music.

The people at work, I get along with a lot of them but a few of them from time to time have wound me up, got me upset and made me angry. Maybe sometimes the guys hassle me too much in the lunch room. Normally I let it go like water off a duck's back, like when I was at school and I used to take a lot of these things personally. The kids gave me a hard time all the time, because they wanted to upset me and see me angry 'cause they thought it was fun. School had its good and bad times. I found third form was the hardest year. Kids gave me a hard time. I had very nice teachers mostly. I had a few teachers that weren't so good but most of them were very good to me, and very understanding. The people are very nice to me at work.

At college I got 'brought up' in the Study Support Centre where relationships and friendships were a big part of it. How to treat others with respect and what the Bible says, 'Do unto others what you will have them do unto you'. I guess in a lot of work environments, I think for a lot of men that can be the opposite. But I'm learning to cope with people that criticize me. I like the ones that understand that we all stuff up at times. I kind of get brassed off with those Christians who think you get saved overnight and then for the rest of your life you're perfect, and I don't agree with that. Even after we're saved we still do dumb things and we're still humans. What we have to understand is that we're all sinners and no-one's perfect.

I mean I don't like to be too judgemental. I don't like to shove it down other people's throats because a lot of Christians love doing that. I feel way too shy. If I went out and did that, I'd probably get beaten up. At the end of the day I just like to do what I feel comfortable doing and being myself, even if it's just setting a good example. Like one day I was driving back through Paeroa and there was this Maori guy walking somewhere in the rain. I picked him up and gave him a ride. You don't have to tell the gospel of

Jesus. Even if it's just doing helpful things, like showing your friendly side and just simple things like that. When I'm angry I don't really think 'friendly', but most of the time when I'm calm and collected I do.

I've had trouble before with understanding my dad's mum. She's 89 now. She's very old and she can't cook. She's got arthritis in her fingers I think. It took a lot of time for me to understand her. There were times when she really made me angry and I would curse at her because she was very awkward at times. At an old age this is a real shame when you get young people that don't understand old people and they start getting very cruel to them. Or maybe if it's someone with Down Syndrome, or in a wheelchair who can't walk, maybe it's someone who can't talk. So really I should be thinking, 'Well, if there are people out there in the world that maybe don't understand me, maybe I've got to think of some people that I don't understand that well.' Because maybe the people who don't understand me, maybe there are a lot of bad things happening in their lives. Like maybe there are some things that they are really struggling with, that maybe a lot of people don't understand them. So it's giving, not taking. You can't always expect people are going to be friendly to you and understand you, so you've got to learn to show your friendly side first if you want someone else to show their friendly side to you. When someone gets angry with me, it's very hard for me to be friendly to someone who's angry with me. It's learning to stay calm.

I find that I can get on a lot better with people. The more they understand me, the more I can get on with them. But then also, I've got to think that, well, maybe if I want them to understand me, I've got to understand them. 'Cause we should all learn to give and take, you know. We can't just take, we've all got to give too. It's not an easy thing to learn to do in life, to give more than take. The Bible says, 'You must give to receive' and so you can't expect that other people are always going to understand you. You've got to understand them at the same time.

FAMILY OF JOHN: 22 YEARS

Mother: John's almost independent. Sometimes when I see him, I think, 'Oh, he's really independent,' because he owns his own car and he drives all over. He drives into the city several times a week. He loves driving. I think it's really good for him. He'll ring me up sometimes in the middle of the day and say, 'I'm just going to visit my aunty' and he'll drive off there which is two hours away. He'll drive somewhere to a beach and go for a swim and then come back. It may be a few hours away. He likes doing things on his own. I think the time on his own driving probably calms him down if he's got things going around in his head.

One of the things that's kept me going is believing in him, because you can have terrible times. I mean there were years where just about every window in our house got broken. Lots of our doors were kicked in because he had a foul, foul temper and there were times when he hit me. There were some really tough times but yet at the same time he was still John. Then he'd switch off and the next day he'd be like it hadn't happened. He'd be excited about something that was happening and was taking each day as a clean slate. There were times where you felt like you could give up but yet knowing that I needed to keep believing in him because

I'm his mother and he is a wonderful boy. He's a man now, but just being able to keep believing in him, just knowing you can put that behind, and you can start again.

John has a part-time job two days a week, that's a paid job. It is under a scheme where the employer gets reimbursed. So he's on a wage but the employer gets reimbursed for some of it which means they're not going to put as much pressure on him to perform which is good. He's been there for several years now. It's a labouring job near his home and then at least three days a week, he works voluntarily at two different railway enthusiast places. One is nearby and for the other he drives up to the city. Again, because they're voluntary, I can imagine that they're not putting as much pressure on him. I think at the moment he wouldn't cope somewhere if he was expected to perform like everybody else at a job, especially under pressure when they're wanting to meet time limits. The temper is still there but it's less often and he talks about it a lot afterwards. If he loses his cool, he's really remorseful. He gets really upset about it and doesn't know why he's done it and talks about it a lot.

John talks now about the different people at the two different railways he goes to. He's had some, I think there's been some grumpy old men, who have told him off because he was meant to paint something and it wasn't super tidy. I mean he's got a lot of learning to do, though. And some of them are more subtle in the way they treat him, and some of them aren't. He talks about the people who aren't patient with him and the people who respect him. He will talk about how at one railway, people trust him to do things more at one railway than the other one. One he started going to when he was quite young whereas the other one in the city, he just turned up and offered his services and I guess they don't know the full history of him. None of them have ever contacted any of us. They just know him in his own right and they've trusted him more than the one that he's been going to since he was a boy. I'm sure they make allowances for him and they've seen him blow his top. He's blown his top at both of them. But the good thing about John is, even if he blows his top, he might not go for a few days but then he'll go back. He'll say, 'I'm sorry' and he'll carry on as if it hasn't happened and they've obviously realized that. But it's interesting that he talks about this. The people at the two railways treat him differently, but he's thinking. He said, 'If I had to choose, I'd stick with the "new railway",' (joined more recently as an adult).

The teenage years were the hardest. I chose to take him out of the Special School and he went to the local high school in the mainstream which was a very difficult decision. It was really hard for him socially but he certainly learnt a lot from it.

He still had teacher aide hours for some of the time and they had a support unit where he could go if he was having a hard day and some days he'd be there all day. Some of the teachers actually were the most difficult part of his schooling. The school got to know which teachers not to have him with. There were some who refused to have him. Technically they weren't allowed to do that but they did. And maybe when the other students saw the way that John reacted, they fed it because it was entertaining. So there were things like that, that were really hard on him. But having said that, some of those people now see him as an adult and they respect him and they see him driving and they see he has a job.

John left school after fifth form. He decided it wasn't the place for him and he went to Polytechnic for two years. It was very good for him. It was the special needs course so it was time management, money management, personal relationship skills. They did work experience, things like that, so it was very practical. Also he had to cope with travelling. He got rides with people and that sort of stuff. So it helped his independence. But he was probably one of the most capable ones there and he knew that. But he made a lot of good friends through there and over the two years he was there, he had three different girlfriends from the course. But a while back someone asked him something about girlfriends, 'Oh no,' he said, 'I've decided girls don't like trains.' So he didn't really see the point. Maybe he'll change his mind. I don't know.

He was talking about Valentine's Day and saying, 'Well, I don't have a partner now' and he'll just change the subject. He didn't really see the need I suppose if they didn't have the same interests. He's actually taken girls a lot on trains, on a train trip. There was one particular girl, she is still a good friend, she went on some train trips with him and to some dinners with men getting up and talking all about trains and things. She was probably bored to bits but she was very sweet about it. I hope for him that he will have somebody who wants to be close to him but it will be a very special person I'm sure.

On Sundays he goes to church. He's become very Christian and that's his own doing. No-one else in the family is or is involved with it. He's got his whole set of friends that know him through church. He's got three different churches he goes to, depending on his frame of mind. Generally he goes to two different ones, one in the morning and one in the evening on a Sunday and he goes to a home group during the week with the other church.

When he had his 21st birthday nearly two years ago, he sent out invitations to 150 people. I suggested that he made lists of people that he wanted to have there. He made a list of people from church. He made a list of people from the railway and people from school. He used to be quite involved with Special Olympics. There were over 100 people there that came. He gave a speech, he sang. It was really quite neat. A lot of people knew him that I don't know and sometimes, like when I go to get my hair done, the hairdresser, she goes to his church, she knows him. She didn't know at first that I was his mother, till we were talking about something and made the connection. So she always tells me about him and how they love having him there, how he sings above everybody else in the church and he's really friendly.

He's very loved and he has a lovely laugh. When I went just last week to get my hair done, the hairdresser said to me, this lady who goes to the same church as John, she said, 'We love having John in the church. Often you can hear him laughing above everybody else if the minister says something funny, and he sings louder than everybody else' and she said, 'They all love having him there.' So that's good. And that's the one he goes to most regularly. I think perhaps the other one, they were a bit more judgemental and he could feel it. A few more expectations of him.

John can still get anxious. Sometimes I wonder if it's a chemical imbalance. Sometimes I think it is because he's tired. When he comes over here you can tell straight away whether he's calm and he's really happy. He comes and he'll be telling you something funny that's happened and he talks very loud. Loud and deep and he laughs really loud. But if he's churned up, the whole way he talks is quite different. I'll listen to him and let him talk and then you get to a point where you have to distract him. You have to say to him, 'John, that's enough.' Sometimes when he talks about things it calms him down, but other times it can churn him up even more. It depends. Hunger I reckon makes a big difference. We went to the beach and there was a fish and chip shop there. We got him some fish and chips and he sat down and ate them and then he was singing. He was as happy as Larry. He's always been more agitated when he's hungry.

Like when he came in the other day when he got back, we went off to the beach, went for a swim, gave him something to eat and then he came right. And that was something that worried me when he got his licence. What would happen if he got angry? But he talks about it and he knows that if he's angry, he's not allowed to drive and he hasn't had any accidents. I was really nervous about going in the car with him when he first got his licence. When he's driving, he doesn't talk much at all. He's concentrating just on driving really, and he drives very carefully and slowly. It's actually more scary going with my eldest daughter in the car.

Getting his licence was a huge thing for him, and getting a car, because then he wasn't dependent on waiting for somebody to take him somewhere and go with him. The teenage years were pretty hard because he was aware then that he was different. He didn't get invited places like the other boys at school and he'd end up going to the movies with his mother which didn't impress him too much. He was pretty good about it but he went through a phase where he could see that's not what the others were doing. But once he could be independent, he actually likes doing things on his own and that's eased his anxiety a lot and he can make choices now too.

John goes to lots of camps. Over the New Year, he went to a Christian camp up north. He takes his tent and pitches it and he sleeps in the tent by himself and that's safest, rather than trying to fit in with other people. That one was about five days. He manages. Well, no-one's rung me up and asked me to come and get him or anything. In fact he chose, too, to take his car rather than go on the bus because he wanted to be independent in case it was too much and he needed to leave. Because sometimes he has problems, like the church, with people who are really dogmatic. He loves music and one of the churches that he used to go to, they told him that some of the music he listened to was evil. We had lots of conversations about that. He seems to have gotten over that now.

He has his own views on things. We do hear his own views and he is allowed to have them, but he struggled. That was one of the things, when I talked about the people at the church telling him something was evil or you have to read your Bible every day. Or some particular sermon he may be upset about. He's very sincere, but he's not going to be a missionary; well, who knows, he might be, but not at the moment, but getting him to understand that it's OK for him to have his own view. I imagine he was hearing at church very set things, 'This is what you have to believe' and the struggle was, 'It's OK that I think differently, but I don't need to tell them that I think differently. I'm allowed to.' That was really hard. It comes back to the Theory of Mind concept. He didn't used to be able to understand that any-body could have a different opinion to himself and, in fact, sometimes he still gets angry: 'How could someone have a different opinion to himself?' 'How could trains not be the most important thing?' But even then, learning to accept that it's OK for him to choose to have a different opinion and from saying what he's been told he ought to believe at church, and accepting that 'it's OK', is something he has struggled with. But he'll talk about it now and he'll say things like, 'Well, when I'm around so and so, I'm not going to talk about music,' or whatever it is that has been an issue in the past.

He's just been on a trip. He quite often goes on excur-sions, train excursions, preferably steam ones. But this one, he was away two nights. One night he stayed with his sister, and the next night in a motel, then he flew back. John can get himself to somewhere on time to catch a train or a plane or those kinds of things. In fact he packs all his own bags before he goes. He's very organized. He might in fact pack his bags a few days before he goes. Not like me.

When he went on this last trip, it was organized through the railways association and most people are going on their own and want to be in a room on their own or going as a couple. But John being John, they put him in a shared room with a 95-year-old man, who's a railway enthusiast from way back. He was obviously travelling on his own and they put John in the room with him. John was telling us this story about how this man had got up five times in the night to go to the toilet and he couldn't see the way. So John had got up and put the light on for him and he said, 'I had to wait for him when he went to the toilet and I couldn't turn the light out till he came back and he was back in bed.' He was tired because he'd been up five times in the night to a 95-year-old man. I thought it was quite delightful. He might not have coped if it had gone on for a week.

He's really caring. Recently with his grandmother (that's my ex-husband's mum, she lives near him, she's 89 now), everyone else was away when it was her birthday. I suggested to him, why didn't he do something with her and he got really excited about it. He took her for a ride on the train for her birthday and he took her out to lunch. He took her to the beach. He drove her around. I was really impressed that he'd done that. The same with my mum, who now has quite advanced Alzheimer's. She used to look after John quite a bit, too, and come and stay and look after him. For a few years when she was getting really forgetful, she'd ask him something he'd already answered. He didn't understand that and he'd say, 'I've already told you.' But now he knows. It's a bit like their roles are reversed.

John does his washing. He lives with his dad but he has to do his washing and he cooks. He's kind of absent-minded. I mean he'll come here, he'll have a meal and he'll get up and walk away from the table and, not purposely, leave a mess. He just doesn't notice that he's left his plate with his food on it. Its not that he's being lazy and it's not that I didn't try when he was younger, to train him to take his plate and put it on the bench. His head is just full of something else. He gets up and walks off and I still have to say to him, 'John, do something about that.' He wants to be independent, he wants to go live in a flat. It would have to be a pretty patient person to live in a flat with him but he's getting there. He's further down the track than he was.

He's very interested in politics, especially as it relates to the railways. He's disappointed that National (Party) got in because Labour (Party) bought the railway back and they were going to spend more money on the railway. But National has withdrawn some and are not going to spend so much money on the railways. If you ask him about that, he'll go on and on and on.

He's very moral. If there's something on the news about child abuse or something like that, he'll say his piece. His sister is politically minded of course, and his dad is, and I'm sure that they have their political debates because his father would be completely the opposite of John. John has his own opinion about things but a lot of it is based on trains and moral things.

He'll go along to meetings if there's something that he feels very strongly about. I remember a year or two back, they closed the forest to the public for a while. At that stage he was really keen on mountain biking. He used to go out to the forest, mountain biking and he went along to a public meeting about it.

He's written two letters to the Prime Minister. One was to do with trains and the other was to do with the drinking age. That was the first one he wrote. He doesn't drink a lot. He'll have one, maybe two beers and that's the most. But when he was approaching, it must have been when he was approaching 18 and they were talking of raising the drinking age to 20 years, he was very concerned because he wanted to be able to be allowed to have a drink legally. He was looking forward to it and he wrote a letter and he got a reply. They didn't raise it and maybe he thought it was because he wrote the letter.

John is happy. Except for when he's churned up, he's really happy and if you see him at a party, he's dancing. He doesn't have to get drunk to enjoy himself. He's a fantastic dancer and he's not inhibited and he loves karaoke. He went through a phase when he'd go down to the local pub and they'd have the karaoke nights so he'd go to those by himself. He went on New Zealand Idol and he was on TV. That was the very first New Zealand Idol. It was a few years ago and they interviewed him and he spoke really well. I've got a copy of that. I was really nervous that he was going to embarrass himself or say something that he shouldn't have said, but he was really good. He didn't believe them when one of the judges said he couldn't sing in tune. He just didn't believe them. He still doesn't believe them. I was worried that he would get upset but he didn't. He took it really well. But he had seen other people coming and going and other people being rejected, but he took it really well. He got to be on TV. He doesn't do it now but for a couple of years afterwards when he'd meet someone he'd say, 'You'll have seen me on New Zealand Idol.'

John's got a neat sense of humour. Sometimes if we go to a movie with him, he laughs a bit after everybody else and if there's a joke, especially if it's a subtle one, people laugh and then you'll hear this loud, deep laugh and you think, 'It's John.' In fact someone once said to me, they realized they were in the same picture theatre as John because they knew his laugh. But he loves funny, slapstick things and things that are blatantly funny and he roars his head off. He's perfectly happy to go to a movie by himself.

He ended up with two unicycles. You probably only knew when he had the short one. We ended up getting one of those really high ones with the chain. We had this contraption with a ladder to get on to, to get on to it. He did the Christmas parade several times, two or three times on the short one, then a couple of times on the high one. But the high, high one was the one we ordered in because he used to go on about high, high unicycles. It's still in the shed. He hasn't ridden them for years now.

My new partner, he's only known John as John now and he knew very little about autism so he just takes John at face value as he is now. I have got accustomed to when my husband and I were separated, if there was something to do with John, I tended to contact my ex-husband and, 'Could you make sure John does such and such,' and he did vice versa and 'Don't forget to remind John to…' We were still doing that and this was only just over a year ago and my partner was asking, 'Why do you do that? Just ask John.' And I do now. I just deal directly with John. But I hadn't even realized that I still did that. Because I've known him for so long and I've always thought that I had high expectations of him but it's hard to completely trust, I suppose, because you know what he has been like and what he can be like. But my partner and I recently went to Australia and John took us to the airport. We were dependent on John remembering and John coming in time to pick us up and I only dealt with John, and he did. He took us to the airport and it was good. But that made me realize that I wasn't treating him fairly. I wasn't giving him all the respect that he needed. Even though I thought I was, I wasn't. I was still mothering him too much. It's thinking, 'I don't need to refer to anyone else, just John.'

I now teach children with a range of special needs, but I've taught quite a few children with autism. There's one little boy that I've taught that's John all over again. He even looks like him. I loved working with him and reminding me of some of the things that John did. Rather than finding the things he does infuriating, I'd enjoy them.

Some children at say five and six that I've worked with, I've been able to see things that they do where I think, 'Oh, that's right. John used to do that.' And when their mum comes in and they're really worried about it, I've been able to say, 'Look, it's not a big issue, because they'll get over it,' or 'It's actually a good thing because it's going to mean that he can stick up for himself,' or something. I can't pinpoint things but you can get a long-term view I suppose. People who haven't seen the progression that I've seen in John (but then not all children with autism have progressed that much), but because I have seen that progression, then I have high expectations for the children that I work with. I expect them to progress as well and I see it in them. I do have to resist saying to parents, 'Oh, he will be able to do this,' because he might not. But yet I'm expecting that he will. I certainly encourage them to have high expectations.

PARENTS OF ALEX: 22 YEARS

Mother: Well, Alex has grown up. She's 22. A year ago she celebrated her 21st birthday at her home and we had over 50 people celebrating that in the backyard. Alex had a Social Story™ (a short story using pictures or photos and text to describe a specific social situation) to help her prepare for lots of people coming to her flat to share the day.

She was up in the morning. She was dressed before anyone arrived. She spent the whole day outside mixing with her family and friends and by mid-afternoon she had taken ownership of the camera. She was busy organizing people so that she took photographs of them. She has taken the most incredible close-ups of their faces but instead of using the zoom lens she simply went right up to their face with the camera. But because people accommodated that and have accepted Alex for who she is, you've got these most relaxed, gorgeous-looking close-up photographs that would make an incredible exhibition. She had an absolutely glorious day.

Alex left school two years ago and she's now living independently from us in the former family home. She shares the house with her older sister who lives downstairs. They're getting on really well together which is really interesting because I thought they'd kill each other when they were teenagers but they've turned out to be pretty compatible.

One of the gifts that Alex has is as an artist. She was lucky enough to meet with a really skilled art teacher when she was at school. What we have is about 12 paintings that she did when she was between the ages of about 12 and 18. She has developed her own business called 'Alex's Art for Hire'. Anyone can hire her paintings for $10 a week and some of the more famous paintings, like 'Alex's Sunflowers' in the style of Van Gogh, we've got printed off. She's now sold three of those prints, one to a very discerning art collector who happens to be Canadian. So we say that Alex is an international artist by repute. We're in the process of developing a website for her, and pamphlets so that people can order her paintings online. The other thing that she has just very recently been successful at is that we put forward a proposal for her to participate in the International Disability Art Symposium which is going to be held in Auckland, New Zealand, in 2009. We hope that she will be one of the artists who will be exhibiting at the Auckland Town Hall. Just this morning we received a telephone call from her old school because last year at Alex's graduation, we thought it would be a great idea if she donated a cup. So this year is the first year that 'Alex's Art Award for unique artistic talent' is going to be awarded. The recipient is going to be a little boy who's in a wheelchair who is starting to lose the use of his arms and legs. But he's painting, using a paintbrush and some kind of holder and he's absolutely enthused. So we didn't want the award to go to someone who produced beautiful paintings necessarily but someone like Alex who produces with 'flair', and the end result is unique. And every year a member of this family, hopefully Alex one year, will turn up to hand that cup over to the person who's won the award. So Alex has a growing reputation as an artist both here and internationally.

What we're trying to do is support Alex to start painting again. The way in which we want to do that is not to get her into some kind of disability art group, but to hire Alex's painting out. To show Alex that her paintings are of value to people, to show her how she might be able to earn money so she understands the connection. It also crossed my mind that the 'Alex's Art for Hire' website could become a place where other artists could advertise their art and that she might get a percentage from whatever sells. Or they might pay for that space while we maintain the website. So that's what we call 'Alex's micro-enterprise', her little business, because we think Alex won't go out to work, even part-time or full-time, but that shouldn't prevent her from having a valued role as someone who owns her own business.

About two years ago we pulled together what people call a 'circle of friends'. We call them 'Alex's advocate group'. They're a group of people who we identified, person by person, to help the family in our thinking. We knew it would be up to us to try and support Alex, to carve out some kind of life, and we knew that it would be too hard to do that thinking on our own.

We try to meet reasonably regularly and that was a really supportive thing to do for us actually. What it means is that your parenting and your decisions are challenged, but they're challenged by people who it's OK to be challenged by. It's not like being in the education or the health system, but people who are there because they genuinely want to share an hour of their lives once every six to eight weeks, to help us make decisions about Alex's micro-enterprise; about 'Alex's Art for Hire'; where Alex is going to live; job descriptions for the support staff; which 'provider' we might be involved with; whether we were going to do it on our own or whether we would involve a provider. All those big, big, big decisions that were just becoming overwhelming to make. I'm pleased we've widened our family circle to include those people. We knew we would have to come up with something highly creative that was responsive to Alex and while we have a long way to go, we've made a good start. A really good start.

I think I would still maintain that Alex's best learning took place when she was in standard 2 and 3 when she was 8, 9 and 10 years of age. She had a very, very good teacher aide who used her made-up approach and Alex learnt to read and write and spell and add. It was just extraordinary how she went about doing that and that gift of literacy has supported her communication into adulthood. You can have a whole 'conversation' with Alex that can take me about an hour and a quarter. She has this stack of paper. She can communicate now with a few spoken words, lots of written words which enables her to have a conversation about what she wants to eat, where she'd like to go, what she'd like to buy, or when she'd like something to happen, or what photos she wants and who she wants the photos of. She does that by writing, Tues 21st of November 10 Kodak photos, with the person's name and basic address. She's big on photographs.

So she's grown up. She's 22. She's independent of us. She's starting to make some really good choices. She's a very good manager for her team. She's a skilled trainer of support staff and she has her home looking the way she wants it. She's happy. So we are learning how to respect her choice to keep her community close to home. We would want her to have a greater presence in her community than what she is choosing to have, but two years after Alex decided not to leave the family home, for whatever reason, I'm beginning to rethink what having a presence in the community means. If it means getting out to the shopping centre, having 'flat white' coffees with your friends, spending money and being part of the sporting group, then that's just not Alex. And there are lots of people in the community who are reclusive, who enjoy their own company, who manage a very small circle of friends. They are very happy doing that and so that's where my thinking is going at the moment. This is clearly what Alex is choosing to do.

What we want to support her in is to have a greater number of people to pop around for a barbecue, just to drive by and pick up some herbs that she sells because she sells herbs and lemons (she sells lemons off the lemon tree), on their way home. Or think, 'I've got a spare hour today, I might just pop around and spend ten minutes with Alex,' because she won't talk on the telephone so that limits things even further. So we really have to think very creatively about how to support Alex to be part of the community.

I like my own company. I enjoy my husband's company. And then it raises the query, why we are so hell bent on getting Alex out there when we're taking our own time to do that. We pick and choose. We're not great socialites.

What people do when they travel, they send postcards to Alex because they know she likes going to the letterbox. They send postcards and keep in contact regularly. People know when they have their photographs taken that they are agreeing to have multiple copies of those photographs forever. They will happily pose now. So people contribute in their small way.

That's mostly it too. As Alex has grown up, she's got this great sense of humour, a really highly refined sense of humour and she's incredibly sensitive. I think one of Alex's greatest gifts and greatest burdens is that we would say she is hypersensitive to criticism. Alex is desperate to get it right. She's always searched for 'how to get it right' and is always seeking confirmation that she has got it right, whatever 'it' is and I'd say she's pretty much got it right at the moment. In her very small world, that's right for her. So we are learning to respect that, to work with it, to challenge where she's at in a really respectful, careful way.

If I reflect on the last 22 years as I can now, there's been huge laughter. We've laughed and that's the one positive thing that I can say over the last 20 years. It has been the loving laughter that's been there for Alex, with Alex, us, and all the incredible people we've met because of Alex. It's been a gift.

PARENTS OF RICHARD: 25 YEARS

Mother: Richard is 25 years old now and he's had two part-time jobs in the last year. They've both been cleaning jobs for about 12 hours a week. I think it's unfortunate that someone as fit and capable as Richard cannot find full employment. He's 6 foot 3 and very fit and is more than capable of working all day for example in the warehouse, unpacking things. He can put things away on the high shelf, he can read and write. He can tap into the computer and he can use Excel as well as type into the computer. A warehouse job in my view would be perfect. I would be happy for him not to earn the full amount a week and he's capable of getting a bus there. And as far as I'm aware he would keep himself safe. The new New Zealand OSH (Occupational Safety and Health) regulations make it very difficult for people to employ people like Richard as well as, of course, the minimum wage.

I guess my main issue these days is that I really do wish that Richard could get full employment and there would be more understanding people out there that would allow him to work. He had work experience at a local company when he was at Tech, and he was packing jelly. He would sit there all day with these lovely Polynesian ladies packing away to their music. He was happy and it was amazing the rate that they could do it at. There's certainly no way I could have packed that fast, but he enjoyed that. Employers actually should take into account the advantage of employing someone such as Richard and other people like that. They speak when they are spoken to. They do exactly what they are told. They don't have private conversations on the phone. They don't spend all day texting and they don't worry all day Friday what's happening Friday night or Saturday or any other day. They don't get drunk and not come in the next morning. They're very rarely even sick. They don't call in with 'sickies'. There are huge advantages of employing people such as this, if employers would only understand.

Richard did continue mainstream education right through to the end of secondary school. He stayed six years at secondary school. The sixth year was probably a mistake in hindsight but it took until May or June to work that out, and by then I thought it was appropriate for him to stay till the end of the year. He was OK still doing PE (physical education) and he was still doing word processing and computer stuff which was good, and he was able to change to his level. He was still doing Correspondence English and maths and I think in the last year he dropped science because by then he'd repeated science so many times, and I didn't mind that. By then my younger son was starting secondary school, and I thought it was appropriate that Richard had left before his brother became compared to him or anything else. He did actually attend the same secondary school as both his brothers.

Richard has been at Tech for two years doing the work skills course. It's a very good course. They're quite confident, they learn at their own ability there and from there he gets assistance to find employment. Since he was 21, he was initially catching the bus to Tech where he walked from home to the bus stop. He's currently catching the bus to his job in the city. The Tech course focuses on life skills, cooking, money. They keep a notebook and they record what they spend that on. Money's probably still an issue with Richard. He knows his PIN number on his card. I just don't trust the other people well enough to allow Richard to use his card. He can walk up to the supermarket and does some of my shopping. It's interesting how he can always work out the price so that there's enough left over to buy himself a Coke or something. So maybe I'm misjudging his ability with money.

At the moment he's going out with a support group. He's been going out with them for about six and a half years and this year that's changed instead of a Saturday night to a Friday night which I think is good. It's more of a social time when people his age would be going out. They take him to ten pin bowling, out for dinner, sometimes movies, they do a variety of things. They may go dancing. They're obviously funded through NASC (Needs Assessment Service Co-ordination) and they're a lovely bunch of guys. We went to their Christmas party the other week.

Richard still lives at home, with the entire family. Both his brothers are still here as well. They take him out and do stuff with him. In fact we are all now very involved with Special Olympics. So just last night I was refereeing Richard's two brothers on the court as volunteer coaches, assistant coaches and Richard is playing. They assist at ribbon days and competitions and my husband does that as well. He provides the sound equipment and the microphone. We are all going out next Tuesday night to the Special Olympic end of year function.

Sport is a good thing for all people in the community and it becomes a social thing for people with the disability and their parents, as it turns out.

I'm pretty sure that Richard is happy in his own right. He will get up and get dressed and go to wherever he's supposed to be that day. He doesn't have any problems with the day, unlike his father. He knows what day it is, he knows if it's a public holiday. The other interesting thing is Richard's job, since we shifted here, has been to put out the rubbish. This is the only house in the street that doesn't have rubbish put out when it is a short week (public holiday). Richard's the only one who knows when Monday is a public holiday and knows not to put the rubbish out on the usual night. It's interesting when you drive out in the mornings; our rubbish is not out and everybody else's is, and that happens every time there's a public holiday.

Richard brings in the washing and he hangs out the washing and he sees it needing to be hung out and he sees it needing to be brought in. I don't know if you ever heard the story where the speech therapist used to have those silly cards, where you're supposed to put in them in a sequence. There was a picture with the window open with the sun shining and a picture of the window open with the rain coming down. Richard was asked, 'What do you do?' and he said, 'Bring in the washing.' The answer was supposed to be, 'Shut the window,' but we lived in a house with the windows opening out, you didn't need to shut the window.

The most recent funny story: my husband, through his church group, has been at a particular course in the women's prison. A lady rang the other night at a particular time when Richard was here by himself. He answered the phone and the lady asked to speak to his dad, and he said, 'He's gone to jail.' You always hear that people with autism take things literally and he obviously didn't have the social skills just to say, 'Dad's not here at the moment, can I take a message?' or 'Can you ring back in an hour,' or 'Mum will be home soon.' He just said, 'Dad's gone to jail.' I said, 'Just as well you didn't tell her he's gone to the women's prison.'

As a family you have to keep laughing too. And I think that's where I enjoy Special Olympics myself. It's a very positive atmosphere and we all laugh. We realize there's other things to life. I think it makes you more accepting yourself. But in other ways it makes you more intolerant.

MOTHER OF JOSEPH: 21 YEARS

Life has definitely got easier but if somebody had told you all the things that you would have to deal with and still be dealing with! You get better at it and you develop systems and supports that make it easier. You come to an acceptance of it so you don't battle and fight to change things that you can't change. I think when they're young, you're in more of a 'try to fix it' mode whereas when they're older, they are how they are and you support and give them the best quality of life you possibly can. You have a team of people and you've got rid of the useless ones and you've stuck with the good ones. You've worked out what works and what doesn't and you don't fight battles that aren't worth fighting. You're not dealing with mainstream any more because actually for Joseph, while I think it's a really good option for parents to have, it wasn't really good for someone like Joseph. So you go to a Special School and that's easier. You just work out a place that Joseph fits into and make an environment and a support around Joseph, not trying to make Joseph fit into something. It's about making things fit for Joseph, not Joseph fit into things and that just goes a lot more smoothly.

You develop a lot of skills really. You don't realize what a well-oiled machine you've become so you actually make it look a lot easier than it is. The same with his caregivers. We're a well-oiled machine, the whole lot of us, and everything is kind of a strategic, military exercise. Not so much now because Joseph is a bit more flexible about things, but still there's a huge amount of 'how you do things' with Joseph that you don't even notice that you're doing now.

Early on in the diagnosis, you can feel like you've failed because you haven't got this normal child that you thought you had. It's really easy to lose your confidence in your ability to be in charge of your child. You get all these professionals coming in and saying that you need to do this, and you need to do that. If you know or think that there's a way that you want to do it, but then a professional comes in and says, 'Well no, you should do it like this,' or 'No, you shouldn't let them do that,' or 'No, you're going to come to the appointment at this time,' even though you know there's a whole lot of reasons why that's going to be a disaster. You feel like you've lost ownership of the situation and initially you can be very easily bossed around by a whole lot of people. So it's really important when professionals are helping support you, that they take the time to let you say what you think and the reasons why you think it, because you might not tell them if they don't take the time to find out.

Joseph is 21 now and I think it was 14 years ago that we last talked to you. He shifted to the city. He has caregivers that I think, probably the last time you interviewed us, we were doing shared care with them in the small township. We had three younger boys and the twins were babies. He was mainstreamed at school then but we found that increasingly difficult once he got into high school because they didn't have the ability to cope with his needs really. It just seemed to be meetings and stresses and disaster all over the place. So he shifted with the same family. They shifted because it fitted in with their older children who had shifted over there. Joseph went to the Special School and that was a breath of fresh air for us because they were very caring, compassionate people, very professional people. Whatever Joseph threw at them, it wasn't a big deal. It was just, 'Well, this is what we do. We help teach and care for people like Joseph.' So that was a very good move.

Joseph still lives with the same couple. Their boys have all grown up and there's one still living at home with them. Their other boys have come and gone so he's had quite a busy boy life with them. He comes home to us every second weekend. He's done that since he shifted to the city. Plus if they want to go for a holiday, he'll come for a five-day stint. We go over for appointments and meetings so it works out really well. I think Joseph is very lucky because he actually has two families that love him very much. I haven't come across any other people who have got the same set-up that we've got with Joseph. If we were to die tomorrow, they would adopt Joseph. They see him like their son except that they respect that he isn't their son, he's our son.

He has finished at the Special School and we transitioned him to a day service in the middle of last year and that has been pretty good. It's quite a good set-up for Joseph because he's non-verbal and there's not many constructive things that he can do. Joseph has a lot of seizures and they've got more frequent as he's got older. He has two or three seizures a week and they're pretty full on. They last for two or three minutes and most of them are in his sleep so that's quite good because he doesn't hurt himself 'cause he just falls down. So he's sort of changed, in that his needs have changed. Before his needs were more the 'very busy' Joseph and now his needs are more the slower Joseph.

He's a bit of an observer and potterer, is Joseph. So we've developed a programme with them of what he likes to do in his day. He gets one-to-one support. Like, 'This morning he goes swimming' so they take him in the car to swimming. Then they go to the horticulture centre and he'll do a bit of gardening. Then they'll go to the library and get a couple of books out. They're just picture books. He doesn't do the whole reading of books. *Hairy Maclary* is still a big favourite. He likes cookbooks because he's still quite passionate about food so he likes looking at the pictures in cookbooks. Then if he's not well, he'll stay at the base a bit and have a little nap on the sofa or just potter, do some art or cooking with his support person. So that's where he's at now that he's 21.

Joseph is part of the community as much as he can be. The fact that he lives with two families I think is really nice. He has a very normal life really. He goes to specialist services in his day but he's very much part of two families so he does have a lot of people in his life that love him. And I've heard people comment, and it surprises you because people say, 'It's great how you give across that Joseph is just part of your family and he just does what your family does and he is valued. He's not hidden away.' And the same with his other family, he's just completely part of the family and you have an expectation that he will be clean and dressed nicely and cared for. When you do things, he is as important as every other person in that group. It surprised me because you think, 'How do you expect us to behave?' But I think probably the person who commented has been a bit involved with mental health and the institution side of it before community placement. I think that it's not something that we've thought, 'We've got to do it this way to show society how they are doing,' it's just, well, how else would you do it? But it's interesting, probably for our generation and the older generation, because it's quite different historically how someone with as high a need as Joseph actually lives with families and is part of two communities. He's not shut away and we go and visit him every now and then. So I think that is a really good thing. It's just that sometimes it sounds good in theory, but the money and support and the quality of service to help make that happen isn't there. We're just really, really lucky that we have the other couple who would do it even if they weren't paid.

For someone with so many inabilities, he is quite a personality, thank you very much. To all his extended family, Joseph is just Joseph, always has been. He might walk out nude into the lounge and it's, 'Oh Joseph, off you go.' It's no big deal. Everybody just understands Joseph and is compassionate to Joseph. He always carries a straw and a plastic bottle everywhere he goes and you have a new appreciation for straws and plastic bottles and everybody does. That's just how his brain works. Why can't he be? As long as it's not scary, it's not dangerous to someone else or offensive, get over it.

You just cope better because even in your own mind you're reconciling things a bit as time goes by. So we just accept things. You still feel sad about things. I used to worry a lot more than I do now but you figure worrying doesn't achieve anything so you just do the best that you can and that's all you can do. We have the faith in God and I think that that for us personally makes a big difference. Because at the end of the day, you just have to think, well, that's all God required of us to do and the things that we can't do, we have the faith and trust that He will look after. So for us personally that makes a difference.

PARENTS OF ELEANOR: 22 YEARS

Mother: In the early days many of our expectations were unrealistic. On the other hand some things have turned out so much better than we thought they might turn out. When you read some books, it's the dreariness, the dreadful grey existence and it wasn't like that at all.

They're all so totally individual. I think in fact, looking back, I have to say, I think it was damaging to read too much in the early days. You have to be so careful what you put into your head. What was described by one woman about her son was so mind-bogglingly terrifying. It gave you a horror of the future, a terrifying endless, bleak, blackness. You have no idea how terrifying it was. Now you think what a waste of time that was. The reality was so different. It was like a kaleidoscope with Eleanor.

Eleanor is at a Special Centre for intellectually disabled adults. It's modern. They're lovely adults and I have my special favourites. The age of chivalry is not dead. It lives amongst the intellectually disabled adults. Eleanor gets the car door opened for her when she arrives. It's one of the young men there, opening the door for her to take her hand to take her in. On the way out, one guy would take her bag and he had it wrestled off him the other day. He was so cross. Eleanor alone at the centre is the most normal looking. The boys think she is wonderful and they are right, she is.

Eleanor, when she was 15, developed epilepsy. The autism now is of course very secondary in terms of our care for her. The vigilance now is because of the epilepsy, it's not because of the autism so much. But I can totally rely on my other two children to do that. Our other children are exceptional young people.

The people at the Centre love Eleanor so they give her a really good time. She goes line dancing and she goes and feeds the ducks at the pond. She's on every outing going. She's still adored by her dad. He totally adores her. He adores the ground she walks on. Totally compatible. She's delicious.

Eleanor with autism is in a very different bracket because she's clever, and this is where autism is so odd. She's profoundly intellectually disabled and has no communicative language that we know of. She understands plenty of spoken language but she doesn't initiate any at all and yet she's as bright as a button. She's clever. She remembers where everything is. They love her at the Centre. They've found they can give her all the cups and saucers and she'll put them all away. She washes, dries, puts them all away, all in rows. They're in the right place at the right time, every time and she doesn't want anybody else in there helping her because they don't know where to put anything so it annoys her.

So she does learn in different ways but she's as bright as they come. Tell her how to do something once, tell her where it belongs and it's going to go there from now until kingdom come. She will never forget where it goes. As simple as that. Which makes her very difficult to place, in fact, in an intellectually disabled setting and they do have to adapt to her. The staff at the Centre were amazed when she was able to do a 1000 piece puzzle in two days. Three staff members took me over to the table and said, 'We can't believe it.' One woman said, 'That would take me weeks!'

Eleanor can do a 1000 piece puzzle. Give her a day if she can be bothered. Eleanor has learnt to knit. Eleanor can do anything actually if she wants to. Eleanor can cook, she can measure. She has beautiful manual dexterity. She has fine motor skills. She is extremely clean about her person. Eleanor can learn anything. It's whether or not she wants to. It's whether she sees the sense in it and with Eleanor it's reminding her to do it. You have to remind her to do every-thing. That's what's the most annoying now. Isn't it wonder-ful that that's the most annoying thing about her?

They're as unique as they can possibly be. Sometimes you have to say, 'She wants to put the last piece of puzzle in, she can do it. It's OK.' Does this hurt us? No, it doesn't. It means a lot to her. She wants to straighten up that particular book. You have to respect that. She loves crushing things up and putting them in the rubbish. You have to try to go with the flow on that one so I give her rubbish in the garden. I ask her to help me pick things up, put them in the bin. Pleases her endlessly. It's finding ways to help her with that particular interest or obsession. How can I make that particular interest work for me so that it doesn't drive me crazy. I wish I'd known more of that when she was younger. I don't know if it would have helped but I wish we could have been more sanguine about not being able to change things and say OK, that's something she's going to want to do. The shredding of leaves for instance, she used to shred all my new plants. Nowadays I give her branches of trees to shred, because she still likes mulching. But I call it mulching now and I give her branches of trees and say, 'Darling, can you do that for me?' and she does. She's happy as a clam. She fills garden bags for me so tightly that the garden man can hardly lift it and she'll pick up every last leaf. There are certain things you have to stop, but you can't stop everything and it's recognizing what is really important to her.

When I look back, the best moments of inclusion for Eleanor socially were run by the Autistic Association. Every fourth Sunday, we took over the gym and nobody else was allowed except families with an autistic child. It meant the rest of the family could all run around with other normal kids who all had an autistic sibling. Everyone could play ball and badminton and we'd set up different areas of the gym to play games and everyone had a cool time. The autistic child could do whatever they pleased. Nobody stressed. That was the best form of socializing as far as I was concerned. Other mothers would say, 'I've made something. Will your child eat that?' 'Oh yes, crackers. Splendid.' Expecting to take your child along to a normal play group is not inclusion. Other people may tolerate them but they actually won't include your child. It's painful. If other people haven't had a disabled child, they won't understand where you're coming from. They don't understand your grief. I can see why people who are deaf want to stay with other deaf people, so that they don't have to be the disabled one. I can see why a deaf community would work. You just get on and be.

Father: I think there has been a change in attitude towards people with differences or disabilities. I think there's a lot more acceptance, more tolerance, acceptance is the wrong word. I think it also depends on the disability. I think there's a lot more acceptance of certain types of disability like wheelchairs and Down Syndrome. I think there's still the lack of understanding about autism because it's so unusual. Because they're all so different. The funny hand movements, the funny walking. It's not that it's not accepted, it's just that people don't understand what it is and I think that's still true.

MOTHER OF KEVIN: 43 YEARS

Kevin is still in the same job. At work, they actually had to ask him this year to take all his holidays that he had accumulated, because of course the union fight very hard for four weeks holidays. He's well and truly owed four weeks, not to mention long service leave. So he took a week a couple of weeks ago and he's going to take three weeks over Christmas.

He's been there now 24 years and hopefully with this economic climate he will be able to stay. As long as he is working, it's so important that they have something to do. Unfortunately because they get lumped in as part of the mental health thing, they are frequently pushed aside as being incompetent and they're not. If you give them a job to do, they do it as long as you keep reminding them or keep them going on something. But it's not because they're mentally incapable, because so many of them turn out to be quite bright and even if they're not quite bright, they're certainly not stupid. Autism is just totally different. I don't need to emphasize that I'm sure.

I think we just simply have to push more and more and more for the fact that they are different.

When Kevin first went to live in a flat, he went in under supervision because we felt he needed someone to supervize him. He went in with three other people originally. One person he has remained with all the time and he has been with him for about nine years now. And then there were three other young men who came and went in the flat.

He went in with people from the mental health system. Now these people, when they are medicated and when they are OK, are just fine. They have their odd ways the same as Kevin does but autism does not belong with people from the mental health system. Autism is something that they are born with but it is not a mental health problem.

We are now in the process of having to remove him and find a small flat which fortunately I have now found. He will be living in a little bed-sit unit with a kitchen and a bathroom. He will be in his own space by himself but he will have neighbours on either side. I'm hoping that this will be the answer, because the constant intrusion from the person with mental health problems has really got at Kevin and left him worrying and anxious. It's brushing off because the person he's been with the longest hardly ever communicates and Kevin's ability now to hold the same sort of conversation that he used to hold is gradually slipping away because he is not getting any stimulation.

It will take him the same amount of time to drive to work from his new home. He's a very competent driver. It's such a strange thing but I suppose it's because it's not mechanical as in nuts and bolts, but it's a set thing and you do certain things and he does it very well. He's a good driver and he drives a lot. And he's taken himself miles away. He's even driven me down to Wellington, 8 hours away, recently. He's a very capable driver.

Kevin is now under NASC (Needs Assessment Service Co-ordination) agency, a local trust, which is absolutely marvellous. I can't speak too highly of the fact that we've got them. They're not creating any miracles, but the whole point is that they have given Kevin a buddy system. A young man comes round and takes Kevin out for a couple of hours or sits and talks to him. It's only been for about three weeks but it's working very well. Kevin obviously feels quite comfortable with him which is good and that's helping him again with conversation, bringing him back to a conversation level. Kevin has four days with his buddy and he works still, and thank goodness he does work. I can't imagine how he would exist without something to be following through. But his buddy comes at about 4.00pm when Kevin gets home from work because he does a very early shift. He starts at 7.00am and comes out at 3.30pm and then he will stay with Kevin up to a couple of hours. He comes in a car so he's probably a local chap from somewhere fairly close by and they either go out for a drive, or at the moment they go down to the beach nearby and walk along the beach and have a chat. But I think it's helping and it's another male in his life somewhere near the same age.

Having the Trust has really, to me, been a breakthrough. Also we've joined PHAB (Physical and Able Bodied agency). They come round and take a group of them out ten pin bowling. They might go back to what is evidently their club rooms and sit around and have a conversation. I don't know how much conversation comes out obviously but it gets some of them talking. But it's for the people who are down and out, or can't cope, or are coming back from an illness, and it's a very good system actually. That's once a week. They do it on a Wednesday, in this area anyway, and hopefully even when he moves, we will still be under the same group. I hope he will, because he's getting used to the people now. NASC agency might have to change his buddy. It depends on how far they travel. But they also offer up other help and I've been told by Autism New Zealand that we'll probably get a little extra help for Kevin. Once he goes in by himself, so that he's totally alone, we might be able to get someone to call in and just check to see he's not drowning under 10,000 plastic bags or buckets of paper.

Now that we have Autism New Zealand it's a huge step forward, because at long last we have somebody who listens and who understands. It's a huge feeling of confidence that we have someone to go to who knows what we're talking about, and that's half the battle. When Kevin was small and when he was first at school, there was so much bickering about whether autism existed that while all the professionals were having their little say, he was growing up. By the time he had grown, nobody knew what to do and they didn't want to start trying, because it was all too much. So at least now we have early diagnosis and early intervention and with Autism New Zealand and the Asperger's Association, the adults can go in and have their say, and have a discussion point, and they're doing wonders. It's only in a small way probably, but they're starting to open the floodgates. What we need now is the wherewithal and, need I ask, the money and the resources, and please, somewhere to let them go to when they are older. By older I really mean from when they are adults, so that they are not left to go backwards because they don't fit into society. It isn't that they don't fit into society because they're mentally incompetent, it's simply because they're autistic.

DAVID: 23 YEARS AND HIS MOTHER

Mother: I didn't care what he was like, as long as he functioned all right for himself in society. That was my focus. But David's gone way beyond that. He's gone way beyond functioning in society. He's now excelling.

When I realized he was autistic, I really got right down to the bottom. I cried for four days as you would for somebody who had died, because you know that person's never going to have the choices or the opportunities that the other so-called normal children have. You get down to that level, then you can only go up from there. Then you've accepted that person as they are. You don't think, 'I want to change him, I want to make him into a normal person.' You accept it's never going to happen. You grieve for what your child could have been like and then you go on and accept them and try to get them accepted into society. Then you fly by the seat of your pants really. You just feel things from David, because he's my child, so I sort of feel what he's feeling. And you go with those feelings rather than thinking, 'I'm going to do whatever with him today, puzzles or speech, or whatever.'

David: They accepted me for who I was. It's understanding. It's knowing this person is different and you're respecting them for it. You're not trying to change them. It's not a disease. That's just something you have to work with. Like together, we dug myself out of a hole. And that's what it's like.

I just found out that I got into the audiology course. It's got all my interests. I enjoy helping people and interacting with people and you can do a bit of research at the lab level or clinical level which I'm quite excited about. Neuroscience is what I've been interested in, how the brain works and you still do a lot of that. I'm into my own hearing and communication because I've been affected by communication disorders, or disorder I should say. I've had experiences of friends who have had deafness. I know that I'll have a really good future as well. There's a lot of diversity and opportunity. I could maybe get into a management role or maybe develop new hearing aid technology. It's just so much better than what I was doing. There was really no future for me in what I was doing. The thing that made it special for me is because I had the personal experience. I don't discriminate people. I know that they're just like you or me. We're just individuals and you can't judge them on that, so you don't. You have to help get them through and it's the experience that I've had.

I've heard that some people have done their thesis on autism so I might even do that.

I went into audiology for a lot of different reasons. One is to do with the fact that it is communication and I've had problems with communication and I sort of know what it's like. And another is, I had a friend I met when I was working at the supermarket before I went to university and he was born deaf. And that's one of the other reasons, personal experience. Just what they cover in the course is what I'm interested in, like physics and technology, and that doesn't really get covered in what I'm doing now, my BSc (Bachelor of Science). I like physiology as well. I've been to a clinic and it just seems right for me. They seem like real nice, friendly, fun sort of people and I feel that is what I would like to do.

In audiology, you also treat the underlying cause and there's a lot of diversity in it too. I like the diversity and there's a lot of opportunities as well. I don't have to worry about employment either. So there's a lot of different reasons. It's all the little reasons that come together. But mainly I just prefer to interact with people. What's more, I don't really want to get stuck in a lab. It just doesn't interest me. It's very tedious and I can't stand it. You'd think someone like me would like it.

Mother: At the end of his 'Biomed' degree, he didn't know what to do. A friend's mother suggested audiology. He looked into it and he thought it suited him down to the ground. Then he kept bumping into people who had hearing problems. It just seemed to be a path. He was thinking of going into medicine but then he thought he would be too anxious.

David: I think I would be capable but I don't think I would enjoy it. My degree is a Bachelor of Science, a biomed degree, and it's basically a whole lot of different papers. The aim of it is to exam the normal function of a human being at a physiological level, I guess you could say, and help the different diseases. I've always been interested in human biology, as to how the body works I guess. It has much more of an impact and you can help people, whereas other things you don't really have that impact. I mean engineering, you still have a large impact with building but you're not directly helping people. I've just always been interested in that.

Mother: One problem he did have this year was figuring out how he could study, because he had trouble studying.

David: Some things I visualize. Things I don't like, I'll visualize it to help me understand. But once I understand it, it's not necessarily visual. Usually how I remember is if there is a summary flow diagram or there's one picture and that will be my cue. If I wrote stuff down, that made a difference. I think half of it was the fact that I wasn't motivated. When I was motivated I wrote things down too and that helped a lot because that's a visual thing, as you say. Sometimes I can remember stuff on the page but not to the extent that I can use it. I can get mixed up with another page or something. A lot of my friends remember things visually like all the details but I don't. I remember the general details but it helps me remember things. It's like a prompt but I don't remember exact details. I might remember a general shape or something. I can visualize. I can imagine standing on the drive now and imagine how it feels, the concrete even. I can do that. Like chess even, you have to visualize the next move. I don't know if that's the same as imagining something but I can do eight moves ahead and imagine it. That would be a reasonable test actually. Ask to imagine something and solve the problem by visualizing it. I could do that easy. I am quite visual actually. Getting on to the motorway from here, I see one step at a time, in a sequence as though I'm walking. It takes a bit longer for me but I need to know exactly where to go.

Mother: It was definitely harder for David to study than it is for his brother. His brother did what I did but David had to do the writing, the listening, the graphs, the whole thing to reinforce. I don't know if that's because you weren't interested.

David: If I can summarize on a single page and I have, like, a central picture and it all links together and it relates to itself, then that can help me to remember. Like, sequences I remember extremely well but if it's disjointed information, it's very hard for me. But if it's in a sequence I can remember it. Like, if it's imagining myself going to the motorway, if it's in a sequence, once I see one thing I see the next thing.

Like with biology, they might talk about some kind of reaction or some process. Processes are very easy for me to remember, just arrow, next step, next step, next step. I can just do all that. It just flows, it does. It's like I've got this clock in my head. I like chronological things in order.

I thought I learnt on my own but I realized I don't. When I actually paid attention to lectures, it made a huge difference.

Mother: You have changed too though. In the beginning I don't think you learnt by listening.

David: But what I can do is I can listen and switch off. But if I listen and I try to remember it, then I can go quite fast. If I write things down when the lecturer does it, then it helps a heck of a lot. Initially I didn't know how that would help but it does somehow. I must be like other people. I thought I wasn't, you know. But it's not true.

Mother: Recently when we were teaching David to drive, we were teaching him hill starts. That's fine, he got those off easy. Braking, changing gear, everything's fantastic. Then he just started driving on the wrong side of the road because I hadn't told him you drive on the left. So he just drove down the right. I could not believe it. I said, 'David, what are you doing? We're going to die,' and he said, 'I didn't know.' He didn't know you drove on the left, never, ever, occurred to him. Yet everything else he technically could do really well because we'd been driving round the cemetery. You would think naturally, because he goes in cars all his life, you'd notice that everybody drove on the left. That was only a couple of years ago.

David: I have two explanations for that. Some things that are intuitive to others are not to me. The other explanation is the fact that if I don't have to do it myself I won't take any notice. Like if we're just driving, I'll never take notice of that fact, of which lane we're on. I'll be thinking of other things. That's the kind of person I am. I'll only learn something if I actually do it. I've always been like that. If somebody just made me talk about something, I won't really care about it until I actually do it.

There is a theory for that, 'mirror' neurons, like when somebody sees somebody else do something, they simulate their activity in their own brain. Maybe that's not happening in mine. I can make myself imagine it but that's obviously harder. Takes a bit more energy, it does.

Mother: There was one thing that was common to David. At Intermediate school, he was really unusual. He did get bullied and his brother got bullied because of David. But David did athletics and he ended up the fastest boy in the Intermediate. Because of that, the kids that used to be bullying you actually thought you were cool. This is what happened to David all the way through his life and then he eventually becomes the hero. Even though they knew he was unusual, they looked up to him because he was the fastest sprinter in the school. Of course they thought of all the competitions he would win for them. Then at the confidence courses on camp, he'd get up there on those high wires way up in the trees, gaily walking along and everybody going, 'Wow David, wow you're cool. How can you do that?' Because he had no fear.

David: That's all gone. I can't do that any more. I don't even like climbing a ladder now.

Mother: And at high school it happened again. He was in the chess club and they ignored him because they thought he was weird. Then he had to stand in for some boy who was sick and he won the competition, against someone, I think, from the Boy's Grammar and David was the hero again and he was accepted. But there was always some sort of saving grace that made them think he was cool in the end.

David: It's kind of unusual looking back all those years. I was like a different person. It's a very strange feeling. It's a good feeling of accomplishment but it's a strange feeling as well because I guess I haven't really changed.

When people thought I was unusual, I guess it was hard to get what you'd call decent or reasonable friends and I always ended up with the odd one. They had something wrong with them in terms of actually caring about other people but I never had that problem. I just had the problem with actually the means of conveying or receiving what they were trying to tell me. But I'm not so much that way anymore. I have more abilities in that way. I've got better friends now, you know.

I didn't have teacher aide support in the high school but in Intermediate I did. But it wasn't really that good. I don't think they really knew my problem. It was at Intermediate and the beginning of high school stages that I had the most intense problems in terms of peer pressure. I remember at Intermediate I couldn't really learn that well because I was sort of hassled and I was concerned about what the other people thought. In the end they gave me the teacher aide but I don't think it was that good. I think I had the intelligence but that wasn't really the problem. It was more dealing with the people. It wasn't that I couldn't learn. It was that I was being distracted by other people. That's why I couldn't learn.

Mother: At the end of high school, his maths teacher wrote in his year book, 'Good luck David. You were always annoying,' because he always used to ask him all these questions, 'Why is that?' 'How do you know?' I don't think anyone else did that.

David: I'm different just in the ways I think, in the way I approach things. I don't just master a particular technique, I go beyond it. Other people don't seem to do that. Like if they study, they just study in one perspective or in one way but I'll look at it in different ways. To me, if you don't look at it in different ways, it's like you're almost a slave. 'Cause you're just only doing it in the way that someone else wants you to do it, but you can do it in perhaps better ways. There are so many things that we just accept.

I realize that there are a lot of assumptions that you have to make in life and you have to accept some of them, but sometimes it can be very useful if you want to improve something. Like me and my dad have a little hobby. We are trying to make alternative fuel in the garage. My dad's got the ability with the mechanics and I've got the basic scientific knowledge and that's just as an example. I just don't want to accept that this is the best fuel that we have now. You can do a hell of a lot better.

Or with music, I write my own music. I like to be creative and do my own thing.

I sort of believe that's better than just copying someone else. Doing your own thing is what is difficult, what is admirable. In terms of how I'm different is that I guess I appreciate creativity more than just following others or just not questioning other things. I like to try to think of alternatives.

I was quite naïve in some ways. That's why I wanted to work for a year because I knew I didn't really know what was going on in the real world. I was about 18 then. It was hard. I knew it would be, but I thought I needed it, you know. I didn't know what I wanted to do when I left school, that was one reason, and I wanted to know what it was like to make money. Give me an idea of the reality of money and the meaning of money which I did learn. There's a lot of education for lots of different things but not financial education and there should be. It's pretty ridiculous.

I enjoyed the customers. I have a natural 'want' to get on with people. As long as you are still yourself, which is quite a complicated thing. I always try to listen to people all the time. I used to anyway, because I knew socially they probably knew better than I did, if that makes sense. But now I'm getting to the stage where I have to listen to myself because you need to know when to listen to other people and when not to.

Mother: I think in the beginning it was more like learning what behaviour is appropriate but now all your behaviour is appropriate and you're just finetuning it. It's what belongs to you.

He went down to Canterbury. Took the plane down there, he took the taxi and organized himself. Found where he was supposed to go, did the interview and flew back home again. That's quite a big thing to do.

Five years ago though you wouldn't have been able to get on and do that on your own. You would have needed to plan out every single little detail like, 'I might get the taxi. I might get something to eat before I get the taxi.' There were never bits of the itinerary that weren't planned.

David: Now I'm the other way round. I can do things on the spot in some ways. Not spontaneous in terms of behaviour, in my activity probably not. But I can sort of jump into something though. It's not necessarily the same thing. I guess spontaneity is, actually, that you're comfortable with jumping into something different which I can sort of do, or jumping into something without analyzing everything. I can do that. But changing my train of thought, that's something I can't do as much. It's like with conversation, I might talk about one sort of thing.

Mother: That's true. If we're driving along in the car and David's got something he has to say to me, it doesn't matter what I say. I could say, 'Look at that burning house there,' and it wouldn't matter. David would continue on with the topic.

David: But now I realize you don't really have to get everything across. It just depends on the scenario of the situation. Just getting everything out is not a good quality conversation. You have to sort of exchange.

Mother: I wonder if David could help your kids in any way, because it's funny, people come up to him. In the trains somebody came up to him. People just seem to do that.

David: There's a boy with a cochlea implant who just started talking to me. I don't know why, he just did that. We just talked about little things, about what he was doing at school. He must have been about 11 years old. I didn't know him at all and he talked to me. I didn't think he'd want to talk to me because Intermediate kids usually don't like it when old people talk to them or are concerned about how they look in front of their peers. So I just let him talk to me. I was drinking an energy drink on the train and he said, 'Are you allowed to drink on the train?' and I said, 'No, don't copy me.' I just asked him about the cochlea implant because I was interested. At that time I was applying for audiology. He said it was an improvement but it seems it still wasn't perfect though. He was pretty concerned about how he appeared with his peers because he asked me if there were any implants that go inside the head that doesn't appear on the outside. And that sort of moved me a bit because before, when I applied for audiology, I never really thought about that side of it. I always looked at it as you fix their hearing and that's the end of the story. But there's a lot of counselling involved.

Mother: I remember when David was at school there was a boy who was autistic and he couldn't talk. David went up to teacher and said, 'He's saying he wants his yoghurt opened,' and nobody knew what he was saying except for David, or what he wanted. He seems to have empathy because of his disability.

When David worked at the supermarket, he didn't have any friends there. He was feeling on his own. He'd go up to the lunch room and there'd be a man sitting there playing chess on his own. So David would sit down and play chess with him. And this went on for weeks and weeks and I said to him, 'Aren't you going to meet him after work?' and David said, 'Well, he never speaks.' I said, 'What do you do?' and he said, 'We just sit there and play chess.' I said, 'Don't you speak to him?' and he said, 'No, not really. I don't have anything to say to him.'

It turned out he was deaf and David was the only person who ever took any notice of him. They actually became really good friends. That was three years ago and now David is doing audiology. It's what I mean, autistic people can help others. It's that thing of, once you become acceptable in society then you can start using it to help others.

David: I've read a few books on autism and the common theme seems to be that a lot of people don't want to accept their children for what they are. And I think that is very bad because they are still a person. I am just different. There is nothing more good and there is nothing more bad about me. I'm just different and you just have to work your way through it and find the good qualities. You can't just abolish something they have. You have to use it and make it into something more acceptable. You can't just get rid of it entirely. And I think that's what Mum's getting at when she says our family is unusual. You're more likely to accept somebody who is unusual. Mum's said to me quite a few times, I'm lucky to have my dad because most men would probably just walk out when I was like that. He accepted me for who I was even though I was completely mad.

Mother: His dad's got a mad streak as well so they just do mad things together.

David: I think the problem is that autism, the name makes you feel as if it's like a medical condition, like a one-word medical condition that you have to fix and eradicate but it's not, it's part of who you are. I'd call the book, 'Autism… It's not just a stereotype'.

Mother: I've got a theory about autistic people. I think they have an overload of emotions that they can't deal with and that's why they shut down. They either just shut down and go into their own world or they deal with it by making it into patterns. They're a lot more emotional than people think. Like David used to be obsessed with power poles because they're all equidistant and I suppose that makes sense of the world, if you're a very emotional person. It's an emotional dysfunction to me.

I met a lot of them when David was young who would just sit and cry. You have to have some emotion going on there if you're just sitting crying. They say they're not emotional but I think it's the opposite. He has empathy with the cat and dog.

David: There have been times when I've been stressed, like recently at exam time when everyone in the family was sick, but I could have not gone through with the exams and not got into audiology.

Mother: Perhaps your autism helped you through that then, because you had that ability to shut down.

David: It can help me and it can be bad for me. You just have to learn how to use it. That's the key. You can focus on things, but I don't want to completely focus on one thing 'cause then I don't worry about the family.

I found sometimes that if I'm in a lot of stress I can relieve it if I get into a routine. I know lots of people like that. Or if I have order or a pattern, like study can sometimes help relieve stress because it's black and white and ordered. But I'm getting less like that, though, now. I'm more into taking risks and trying different things, because I'm getting sick of the same things. I'm getting stagnant. People need diversity. You need variety. That's important, that's the nature of humans, to try different things. I'm getting to that stage anyway.

I try to use stress to drive myself to get things done. I usually worry about things that I feel that I don't have control over, but if I have a lot of anxiety I usually try to think to myself, what can I do about it, so I try and do as much as I can. As long as I know I've done my best, or I've done something towards it, I usually feel better. I try to make it into a problem-solving thing otherwise it's just a whole turmoil of emotions. What was the sort of autism that I have?

Mother: You were what I would call the classic sort. In the book, every symptom was you, except for the fits. You never had fits, but every other one I could have ticked.

David: I believe I'll go further than where I am now. I'm happy going into audiology but I do have a lot of ambitions. I've always had this feeling that I know that I'm different. You could compare that with people who become religious.

It's like that kind of feeling, that's why I've gone into church. I've decided to see if it's got something to do with God.

I've always felt like I can make a contribution or do something that no-one else will ever do. I'll be a pioneer of something but I don't know what it is exactly. I'll have to explore it. There are a lot of things I don't know about myself. No-one ever really knows themselves anyway. But there's a lot of things I still need to discover.

I do believe that autistic people have an enormous amount of potential, like they do have creativity. I do believe that and they think of things differently. If they could just be helped to, not just to get over their problems, that's obviously the most important thing, but I'd like to see their potential. I can see their potential. I'd like to see that harnessed.

We see things differently and that's an advantage in the end. Because if everybody does something the same way, you're just competing with everyone else. But if you have something different, then you have the edge and that's what usually makes people very successful. You get great scientists or musicians or anything, but not necessarily those things.

You'd think that for an autistic person, maybe a clinical career would be something way out of their reach. That's the impression, you know. But it wasn't for me. I think it's quite good and it's probably something that you should mention in your book, because at least it would inspire other families to not just think of autism as a stereotype. I don't think it is. It's a lot more complicated than that.

I haven't told anyone at the university that I'm autistic. Your capabilities are not restricted to a stereotype. If you believe that you can do more, then you probably will do more, and that's what's been happening at the moment.

Index